SLAUGHTERHOUSE

Gail A. Eisnitz
with a new afterword by the author

SLAUGHTERHOUSE

THE SHOCKING STORY OF GREED, NEGLECT, AND INHUMANE TREATMENT INSIDE THE U.S. MEAT INDUSTRY

Prometheus Books

59 John Glenn Drive
Amherst, New York 14228-2197

Published 2007 by Prometheus Books

Inquiries should be addressed to
Prometheus Books
59 John Glenn Drive
Amherst, New York 14228–2119,
VOICE: 716–691–0133, ext. 210
FAX: 716–691–0137
WWW.PROMETHEUSBOOKS.COM

13 12 11 10   8 7 6 5

Library of Congress Cataloging-in-Publication Data

Eisnitz, Gail A.
    Slaughterhouse : the shocking story of greed, neglect, and inhumane treatment inside the U.S. meat industry / by Gail A. Eisnitz ; with a new afterword by the author.
        p.   cm.
    Originally published: 1997.
    Includes bibliographical references and index.
    ISBN 978–1–59102–450–7 (pbk. : alk. paper)
    1. Slaughtering and slaughter-houses—United States. 2. Animal welfare—United States. 3. Meat inspection—United States. 4. Meat industry and trade—United States. I. Title.
    TS1963.E37   2006
    364.1'87—dc22   2006022924

Printed in the United States of America on acid-free paper.

Contents

Part Two: The Stickers' Confessions

Part Three: The "Slaughterhouse Eight"

Part Four: USDA Deregulates: Full Line Speeds Ahead

Part Five: Friends in High Places

Part Six: A Debased Side of Human Nature

Acknowledgments

I would like to express my heartfelt thanks to several individuals without whom this book would not have been possible. To Bradley Miller and the entire staff of the Humane Farming Association, I am indebted to you for your guidance and for providing the means to turn this slaughterhouse investigation into a book. To Suwanna Gauntlett and the Trustees of the Barbara Delano Foundation, thank you for your unwavering support of this project.

I would like to express my sincere gratitude to Prometheus Books Editor-in-Chief Steven L. Mitchell for having the foresight, courage, and commitment to champion this controversial issue. I am also genuinely appreciative to Associate Editor Mary A. Read for her sensitive nurturance of this book through the editing process.

To my parents, sister, brother-in-law, and nieces Jessica Whitney and Amanda Rachel, thank you for holding my hand and encouraging me through what seemed to be an endless project and the medical nightmare that ensued. To Scott McVay and the Geraldine R. Dodge Foundation, my sincere thanks for ensuring that this material reaches the largest audience possible. To my friends Lisa Landres, Carolle Yamada, Connie Cosler, Bob Baker, and Ellen Truong, I could not have done it without your support.

To friends and colleagues Dr. Stephen M. Kritsick, DVM, and Jolene Marion, Esq., who, although no longer with us, dedicated their entire lives to improving the plight of animals, you have served as an inspiration for me.

And finally, my deep-felt gratitude goes out to all the courageous slaughterhouse employees—men and women, corporate and federal workers—who warmly welcomed me into your homes and lives, patiently answered my innumerable questions, and allowed me to tape-record our many conversations. I am profoundly grateful to you for your brave willingness to go on record on tape and in affidavits, putting your jobs at great risk, so that the public might someday know what takes place behind the closed doors of America's slaughterhouses.

PART ONE

OPENING THE SLAUGHTERHOUSE DOOR

Prologue

The men Carol Taylor dates all seem to have at least one tattoo and hair that's either razor short or very long. She hangs out with crooks and brawlers in bars and roadhouses, and has been chased at 120 mph in the middle of the night by thugs trying to kill her. When stopped by the police while driving with a phony license, she managed to sweet-talk her way out of trouble without arousing suspicion in the man accompanying her—the violent felon she was scamming with the fake ID.

Right now Carol Taylor is sitting with a man she met an hour ago, the cop who caught serial killer Ted Bundy. They are in the Florida mobile home of Gibb and Jean Gibson,* the four of them drinking Scotch and telling jokes.

*Some names of individuals have been changed throughout this book to protect privacy.

The Gibsons train greyhounds to race. Carol Taylor, among other things, is an artist, and has sketched some of the Gibsons' dogs. She opens her portfolio and shows them the progress so far on a drawing of their prize hound.

The Gibsons like Carol Taylor. They've welcomed her into their circle and think of her as a dear friend. Carol Taylor, for her part, is right where she wants to be. She thinks of the Gibsons as the people she's about to have arrested.

I, Gail Eisnitz, prefer to spend my evenings at home with my cat, a cup of tea, and a good book. "Carol Taylor" is my undercover identity and persona. I have been working on and off for months to have Gibb Gibson arrested for the torture and death of thousands of rabbits used as live bait in his dog-training business.

At five-thirty the next morning Jeannie Gibson is cooking us breakfast inside the trailer. Outside, my "boyfriend" Capt. David Lee and I watch Gibb tie a live rabbit to the track's mechanical arm. Some of the country's leading greyhound owners are standing at the edge of the track to see how this round of training goes.

The arm takes off around the track and the dogs leap after it, battering and biting at the helpless rabbit dangling from it upside down. I'm shooting photos as fast as I can—supposedly of the dogs, for portraits, but actually of the people.

Captain Lee ducks his head to speak into his shirt collar. "Takedown. Takedown."

Seven police cars come tearing down the road, and ten officers move out from behind trees around the track. I slip away, ostensibly to point the police in the direction of the evidence, but mainly because I don't want to face the Gibsons.

After the court releases Gibson and the others on their own recognizance, pending trial, the Gibsons spot me Dumpster-diving for more evidence close to their dog track. They pull over, shaking their fists and screaming obscenities. We're all by ourselves on this lonely stretch of road, just me and my former friends. Then Captain Lee pulls up.

The Gibsons drive off, yelling at me as if they would beat me to a pulp first chance they get.

The Gibsons aren't the only reason I'm in Florida. As Gail Eisnitz, I've also come to interview a man named Timothy Walker who has written me a letter claiming firsthand knowledge of atrocities so horrific that I would have dismissed them as ravings if it weren't for his sane and sober tone.

His letter will start me on an investigation that will nearly kill me, an investigation into cruelty so deep and broad, to humans and animals, that it touches every person in this country.

1

One Man's Cry for Help

Timothy Walker is a troublemaker.

In the 1980s, when employed as a Kansas City weights and measures inspector, he found that for the previous thirty years gas stations had been shortchanging their customers. Instead of keeping his mouth shut like everyone else, he blew the whistle. The case made headlines all over Missouri.

Later, as an energy auditor for the city, he tried to get officials to do something about the poverty he saw in the course of duty. The city, claiming budget constraints, refused to act. Walker ended up buying storm windows for low-income families out of his own pocket, paying one elderly woman's real-estate taxes, and bringing Thanksgiving dinner to another.

I first heard of Timothy Walker back in 1989 when, as a field investigator with a Washington, D.C.-based animal protection organization, I received a letter from him. He wrote that he had firsthand knowledge that Kaplan Industries, a slaughterhouse in Bartow, Florida, was skinning cattle while they were still alive.

Skinning live cattle? As a cruelty investigator, I would sometimes receive crank letters about cows butchered by aliens, or messages channeled from manatees, or telepathic chickens. But something about this letter seemed genuine.

"This is not only extremely cruel," he wrote, "but also very dangerous for the plant personnel who have to skin these kicking animals." Plant management knew about the problem, he said, but didn't want to correct it because that would mean slowing down the production line. "I have contacted a number of federal agencies but have been told there is nothing they can do. They also told me that the problems I described exist all over the country, that they are just a little worse at Kaplan's."

᯿   ᯿   ᯿

In my line of work, I've seen just about every imaginable kind of cruelty to animals, from the mundane to the exotic: dogs trained to rip each other apart for the amusement of people, the loser killed and the "winner" horribly maimed; ritual sacrifice of chickens, goats, sheep, and cattle; cockfighting, where birds wearing razor-sharp spurs fight to a slow, bloody death; puppy mills where inbred, genetically deformed puppies suffer from overcrowding, malnutrition, exposure to the elements, disease . . .

But who in their right mind would attempt to skin conscious cows, particularly right under the noses of United States Department of Agriculture (USDA) meat inspectors? Sometimes involuntary reflexes in stunned or dead animals can look like conscious kicking. And there was always the possibility that Walker might not be telling the truth. Perhaps he was just a disgruntled employee. I needed to dig deeper.

❀   ❀   ❀

I learned that Kaplan was slaughtering about six hundred head of cattle a day. Not as many as some of the nation's newer high-speed mega-operations, but still high enough to make it the largest beef slaughterhouse in Florida. Next I called the USDA and requested an immediate investigation. Four days later a USDA official called me back with her findings. She said that no cattle were being skinned alive at Kaplan.

"Though I wouldn't have been surprised if they were, at *that* plant," she added.

"How come?" I asked.

"Oh, they have a reputation around here."

"Reputation for what?" I asked.

She wouldn't elaborate.

❀   ❀   ❀

I decided it was time to contact Walker by phone. He was soft-spoken and articulate. When I asked for the source of his inside information, he admitted it was himself. He was, as it turned out, a USDA employee.

Unlike USDA meat inspectors who examined carcasses and body parts elsewhere in the plant, Walker worked in what's known as the "blood pit." Part of Walker's job was to take blood samples from cows to test for bovine brucellosis, a highly contagious disease which causes abortions in cattle and has a major financial impact on the beef industry. He was stationed on a catwalk between two head-skinners and a man who used a pneumatic dehorner and huge cleaver to cut off the animals' horns and front legs.

In theory, cattle in a slaughterhouse are either prodded along a chute into a "knocking box" or up to a conveyor/restrainer, which then carries them up to the "stun operator." The stun operator, or "knocker," shoots each animal in the forehead with a compressed-air gun that drives a steel bolt into the cow's skull and then retracts it. If the knocking gun is sufficiently powered, well maintained, and properly used by the operator, it knocks the cow unconscious or kills the animal on the spot.

The next man on the line, the "shackler," wraps a chain around one of the stunned cow's hind legs. Once shackled, the animal is automatically lifted onto a moving overhead rail. The cow, now hanging upside down by a leg, is sent to the "sticker," the worker who cuts the throat—more precisely, the carotid arteries and a jugular vein in the neck. The sticker makes a vertical, not horizontal, incision in the animal's throat, near where the major vessels issue from the heart, to cut off the flow of blood to the animal's brain.

Next the cow travels along the "bleed rail" and is given several minutes to bleed out. The carcass then proceeds to the head-skinners, the leggers, and on down the line where it is completely skinned, eviscerated, and split in half.

That's exactly the way it's supposed to be done, according to federal law. But according to Walker, that's not at all what was happening at Kaplan Industries.

※   ※   ※

In 1906 Upton Sinclair published *The Jungle,* an account of an immigrant family's struggle to survive amidst the appalling conditions of Chicago's stockyards and slaughterhouses. *The Jungle* revealed slaughterhouse conditions so shocking and meat so filthy that meat sales plummeted more than fifty percent and President Theodore Roosevelt personally crusaded for enactment of the Federal Meat Inspection Act of 1906. That law and subsequent legislation established standards for plant sanitation and required federal inspection of all meat shipped interstate or out of the country.

Today, USDA employees inspect meat in much the same way as they did back in 1906. According to federal law, all animals in slaughterhouses must be examined before and after they are killed. These inspections are conducted by government veterinarians or trained inspectors. Veterinarians, knowledgeable in animal physiology and health, have general oversight in slaughterhouses. Inspectors, who receive classroom and on-the-job training, learn how to detect lesions, signs of illness, and contamination in animals.

During antemortem (before death) exams, inspectors observe animals in pens prior to slaughter and segregate unhealthy or "suspect" animals for examination by USDA veterinarians. They look for anything that deviates from the norm: animals that can't walk; those with abnormal gaits, tremors, paralysis; those that grind their teeth; and the like. They also look for signs of infection, recent surgeries, etc.

Most inspectors, however, work inside the plant where they conduct postmortem (after death) exams. Stationed in a few key places along the "disassembly" line, they are supposed to inspect each animal's head, carcass, and internal organs for signs of disease, abscesses, and lesions, as well as

Cattle Slaughter

▲ Cattle
driven to
knock box
or restrainer . . . .

. . . animal receives blow to the
head from captive bolt device ▲

. . . is shackled,
hoisted,
and stuck . . . . ▲

Illustrations by Rob Barber

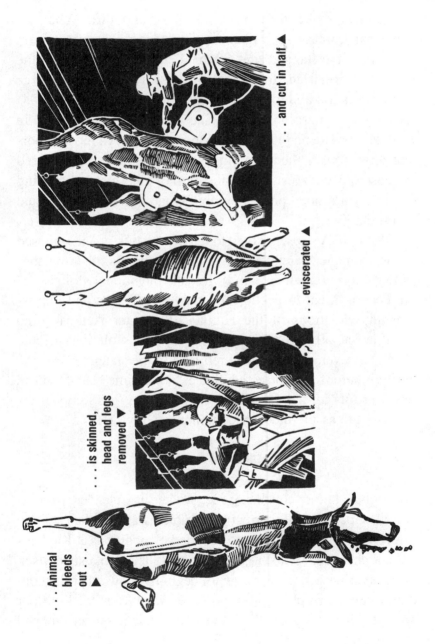

contaminants like fecal material, hair, and dirt. When an abnormal carcass or organ is detected by a postmortem inspector, it is tagged and retained for examination by the USDA veterinarian. Inspectors are also required to enforce plant sanitation and meat-labeling standards.

Congress passed the Humane Slaughter Act (HSA) in 1958 and broadened it in 1978. Among the HSA's most important provisions is the requirement that all animals be rendered unconscious with just *one* application of an effective stunning device by a trained person *before* being shackled and hoisted up on the line.

The USDA, closely allied to the meat industry and opposed to the Humane Slaughter Act, was nevertheless made responsible for its enforcement. And while the intentional violation of the Federal Meat Inspection Act carries stiff fines and imprisonment, violations of the Humane Slaughter Act carry no penalties at all. When inspectors observe violations of the HSA, however, they are required to stop the slaughter process until violations are corrected. Since "down time" can result in fewer profits for the day, the threat of USDA line stoppages is supposed to assure industry compliance with the law.

❋   ❋   ❋

For months before contacting me, Walker had pleaded with his USDA supervisors to correct the problems at the plant. "I can safely say someone is going to be killed if conditions at Kaplan's are not changed," Walker had written in a letter to a supervisor. To another he wrote, "You cannot begin to know what the conditions are at this plant unless you have worked on the kill floor and seen them for yourself. I have almost had my clock stopped [been killed] a number of times by live cows kicking wildly as they were skinned while still conscious." To a third supervisor he wrote, "The situation calls for immediate action. I dislike bypassing the chain of command, but I have now become more upset about the persistent conditions at this place and the inability of the federal government to correct them."

Nothing happened.

In his first effort to seek help outside the USDA, this former navy sailor wrote to the Veterans Administration (VA). "What I saw when I walked into the plant looked like illustrations for Dante's *Inferno*. Hell can't be any worse than what exists at this place."

Nothing happened.

After striking out with two federal agencies, Walker wrote to me.

2

Will We Get Out of Here Alive?

Timothy Walker lived in Naples, Florida, a sunny town sandwiched between the Gulf of Mexico and Big Cypress Swamp. I met him in a small seafood restaurant. He looked to be in his late forties, of average height and build, with glasses and a beard, and a pleasant, self-effacing air. To get acquainted, we swapped a little personal information before I turned on the tape recorder.

Having dreamed of living in Florida, Walker had left his job as an energy auditor a year earlier and moved south. He thought he'd lined up a job with the USDA's animal welfare division, the unit that inspects conditions in research labs, commercial dog-breeding establishments, and zoos. He never expected to find himself inside a beef slaughterhouse collecting blood samples.

"Last Saturday," he said, "the line was smoking. There were more live cows coming through than I've ever seen before. The skinners were cussing. We were cussing. The whole line was going crazy. Just about every cow that come down the line—at least a hundred of them—was alive that afternoon."

According to Walker, while Kaplan slaughtered only fifty to seventy cows an hour, the facility was dilapidated and the equipment too poorly maintained to handle even that many. As a result, when the line speed was increased—particularly when the foreman was trying to push through as many cattle as possible at the end of the work day—plant employees just couldn't keep up.

"The knocker doesn't always hit 'em square," Walker said. "Sometimes the cow will get up and run through the plant. One time I saw a cow come barreling down and knock this Mexican fellow to the floor. Ran right over him. I asked the guy if he was hurt. It was pretty plain his back was killing him but he said, 'No, no.' He knew Kaplan's would fire him if he complained."

A birthday celebration at a nearby table interrupted our conversation. After the candles were blown out and the clapping died down, Walker recounted two other incidents in which USDA employees themselves had nearly been trampled to death by supposedly stunned bulls.

More often, he said, improperly stunned cattle regained consciousness after they'd been shackled and hoisted onto the overhead rail. In addition to kicking and thrashing as they hung upside down, he told me, "they'd be blinking and stretching their necks from side to side, looking around, really frantic."

Regardless, the cattle moved down the line to the sticker.

"A lot of times the sticker just can't do his job right," Walker said. "He doesn't get a good bleed." Still, within seconds of being stuck, the cows arrived at the two head-skinners, who stripped all the hide from the animals' heads.

"A lot of times the skinner finds out an animal is still conscious when he slices the side of its head and it starts kicking wildly. If that happens, or if a cow is already kicking when it arrives at their station, the skinners shove a knife into the back of its head to cut the spinal cord."

This practice paralyzes the cow from the neck down but doesn't deaden the pain of head skinning or render the animal unconscious; it simply allows workers to skin or dismember the animal without getting kicked.

The restaurant was filling up for dinner. Walker had finished the sandwich he'd ordered and I'd eaten my salad. We'd been talking for about an hour and needed a break. We took a short walk along the waterfront, then drove back to my motel where I started the tape rolling again.

"Skinning live animals isn't only cruel," Walker said, "but it's also really dangerous for the skinners and the rest of us." Crammed together on a rusty old catwalk, workers had no place to take cover when live cattle were struggling and kicking on the rail. Sometimes animals would break free of their shackles and come crashing down headfirst to the floor fifteen feet below, where other men worked.

"It's a miracle that nobody's been killed. There were three in one day, one right after another. One hit a worker, just a glancing blow, broke his leg. I almost got crushed by a falling bull."

"So when you decided to do something about it, where did you start?" I asked.

"I asked my boss if I had the authority to stop the line. He said it was Dr. Tecsan's problem [the USDA veterinarian at Kaplan]. 'She's in charge.' In order to tell Tecsan I'd have to leave my station, and if I do that, I'm not taking blood samples. So I'd tell her after I got off the line that they were skinning live cows. Sometimes she'd say something, sometimes she was too busy." Walker named about twenty different people he'd contacted at the USDA, the VA, and the U.S. Congress. "I even contacted Senator Bob Graham [D-Fla.]. At the time, I didn't know he owned a big dairy.

"There's other things, too," he continued. "Safety violations. A lot of times the sewers will stop up, with legs, ears, things like that. The blood coagulates, it backs up. It'll be up to six inches deep, you can't see the drains and you can trip. And sometimes broken shackles—they weigh maybe thirty pounds—fall from the rail and hit workers down below." By the time we finished talking that evening, we had tallied up fourteen different federal humane and safety regulations that were routinely violated at Kaplan.

☀ ☀ ☀

It was tough sleeping that night. First of all, I had a knot in my chest and a sore throat that was keeping me up. Second, as a cruelty investigator I thought I'd developed a pretty thick skin, but this situation at Kaplan was getting to me.

☀ ☀ ☀

The next morning I drove north to Frostproof to speak with Kenneth Sandborne, one of Walker's co-workers. Sandborne, like Walker a USDA brucellosis tester, told me that all the problems on Walker's list had been around long before he'd come to work at the plant. When I pressed him for details and for observations of his own, he told me a story.

Before Walker had even hired on with the USDA, Sandborne and another brucellosis tester had stopped the slaughter operation at Kaplan when conscious cattle were being skinned alive. The plant vice president rushed out to the floor.

"He chewed us out," Sandborne said. "Said we weren't there to stop the line, and if we didn't like what was going on we'd be asked to leave. I don't know how he could threaten us with our jobs when we didn't even work for the plant. We worked for the USDA—the government." Nevertheless, Sandborne had backed down.

Still afraid that he might lose his job, he didn't allow me to tape the interview, wouldn't commit to signing an affidavit, but did say enough to corroborate Walker's statements.

❋   ❋   ❋

Over the next few days, I spoke with two more brucellosis testers who'd been temporarily stationed at the plant. The first tester, Ronnie Watson, lived with his wife and children on a pretty farm in the Florida countryside. When I arrived, he was painting a trailer next to the house. We sat on the lawn. With the family horse looking on and a kitten rubbing up against my feet, I asked him about Walker's statements.

"Don't get me wrong. Tim's good people, but he's out of his element." Watson spoke slowly with a Southern twang. "Nobody likes to see animals hung up alive, but Tim's too sensitive to the animals' suffering. Me, I was scared. I got whacked a few times.

"And it's not just the kicking. I can live with the kicking, it can only hurt you so bad. To me, the scariest part is when the animals fall. A ton of bull falls on you and you're dead. When I see the shackle wheel jumping off the rail, I scatter like quail.

"My wife was scared to death that I wouldn't come home from work in one piece," he said. "I was sure glad I had life insurance when I worked at Kaplan."

I asked if he was sure the cows were really still alive.

"Kicking can be muscle reaction," he said. "If they're bellowing or making noise they're alive. When the eyes are blinking and you've got eye movement, they're alive. And when them things get up after they've been knocked," he continued, "believe it or not it's funny. Everybody runs and jumps like a bunch of monkeys, climbing on things everywhere. It's scatter city."

"Did you complain about the live ones?" I asked.

"I complained to Dr. Tecsan two or three times. I'd say, 'Dr. Tecsan, the cattle are coming in alive. They're dangerous!' She'd go and chew out the knocker, but that wouldn't solve the problem. I wrote a letter—a lot of us wrote letters. I brought it up to Dr. Mitchell, and he told Dr. DeCarolis to get down there and see what the problem was. Dr. DeCarolis comes in in his white uniform and he acts like, yuck. Well yeah, yuck, but I have to work here. He stayed maybe forty-five seconds, then asked me to move a bloody carcass out of his way so he wouldn't get any blood on him when he left."

☙   ☙   ☙

After being confronted with letters and complaints about conscious cattle, USDA supervisors initiated a "study" of the problem. They didn't address humane violations or the dangers of conscious cows on the rail, they didn't slow down the line. Instead, they'd erected a metal plate overhead. I asked a fourth brucellosis tester about this metal plate.

"When I worked at Kaplan's I was told about a protective shield that was over me. I thought everybody was crazy—I didn't know what the hell they were talking about. I didn't see any shield. Another bleeder told me a little metal plate was supposed to keep shackles from falling on workers. It could hardly have saved us from kicking or falling cattle. In reality, there was nothing to protect us but a 'Watch out! Back up!' when the head-skinner started skinning out a live cow's head. But I was grateful he said that. It gave us a chance to get ready for kicking and falling cattle. Sometimes he'd warn us by saying, 'Going to the hospital, going to the hospital.'

"Under normal circumstances I could see Tim's point about cruelty to animals. But not this time. I was too busy worrying about myself to think about the cows—I was thinking, God, will I get out of here alive? One veterinarian, Dr. Tecsan, was absolutely furious."

"About the conditions?"

"No-no-no. That Tim had written a letter."

❈   ❈   ❈

Herb Howser, another USDA contact I'd gotten from Timothy Walker, had been injured earlier in the year while dodging an improperly stunned cow. He *wanted* to be interviewed. When I called him the night I arrived in Naples, he immediately backed up Walker's accusations, suggested he'd be adding some of his own, and agreed to meet me.

Now, just a few days later, I called to confirm our appointment and his voice was as cold as ice. "I don't know why the plant's problems are any business of yours!" he shouted, then slammed down the phone.

I talked to Walker to find out what had gone wrong. He didn't know for sure, but he could guess: USDA brass had interrogated Walker earlier that day about his contact with me. Maybe Howser had heard about it. When we'd initially spoken, Walker had expressed fear that he might be fired for speaking with me. Until now, I'd viewed his concern as melodrama.

Herb Howser changed my mind about that.

3

The Darkest Place
in the Universe

The Whistleblower Protection Act of 1989 is a federal law designed to safeguard government employees from retribution after they expose illegal, corrupt, or improper conduct. I went back to Washington in connection with another investigation, and contacted the Government Accountability Project (GAP), a public interest legal advocacy group that defends government and corporate whistleblowers. GAP agreed to take Walker's case should he be fired for talking to me.

While at GAP offices, I saw a memo to all staff from Tom Devine, the legal director, headed "This is why we do what we do." The memo quoted Mary Heersink, a mother of four from Alabama, who'd spoken out at a USDA hearing in Atlanta. She described what had happened to her twelve-year-old son,

Damion, after he ate a marble-sized piece of raw hamburger at a Boy Scout cookout.

> I have been to what has to be the darkest place in the universe. It's the place where you watch your child's body convulse, his face turn blue under a tangle of respirator hoses, the monitors above him screaming out the alarms as they flash blood pressure numbers. 60/40 . . . 50/30 . . . 40/20 . . . falling, down, down. . . . Then doctors race in with a crashcart shouting at you to leave. They are merciful, they know that parents shouldn't have to see what happens next.
>
> The darkest hour is in the hall outside the intensive care unit where you hold your shaking husband as both of you beg: Please let us keep him. Please let him stay another hour. We're not asking a day, just an hour. Please, God, please.
>
> And you wait. Like you waited during the first week of this hell, like you'll wait for six more. Six weeks of excruciating drama—torturous suffering for him, life-threatening damage, seven times kissing him good-bye as you give him to the surgical nurses who can't believe he can keep up the battle. Six weeks of doors slamming shut on his life, yet doors somehow reopening until God gives His answer: This child is granted a reprieve.

Her story touched me. And while it didn't explicitly involve animal cruelty, I felt Mary Heersink's ordeal was somehow connected to what I was working on. I called her.

After she'd thanked me for my concern, I asked her how her son had come to eat raw meat at a Boy Scout cookout.

The little chunk of hamburger, Mary said, was on a platter that Scouters were using to carry patties to the grill and take hamburgers off. Although it was uncooked, it had turned gray from exposure to the air.

"As soon as my son popped the little morsel into his mouth, he could tell it was all mushy and raw. He told me he'd been too embarrassed in front of his friends to spit it out.

"Exactly six days later, all hell breaks loose. It started with bloody diarrhea, then his platelet level dropped. He was hallucinating—he didn't recognize us any more. Then his kidneys shut down and he required dialysis. That required one surgery.

"Then his lungs became a problem. He was put on a respirator because his lungs were filling up with fluid and tubes were punched into his chest to drain the fluid off.

"And then his heart became involved. It enlarged grotesquely. X-rays showed it two-and-a-half times the normal size. Three times the doctors went in and drained off the fluid around his heart. They couldn't believe they got a whole liter each time. 'This will take care of it,' they'd say. 'We got it all.' Next day, boom, it's back again. They gave up on that and threw him into surgery. That's when they wanted to go in and cut a window in the membrane around his heart. When they got in there, the sac was so shredded and full of pus, they just stripped the whole thing off."

Doctors estimated his chances of survival at one in four.

The hamburger Damion had eaten was contaminated with a deadly strain of bacteria known as E. coli 0157:H7. This germ, which can bring on varying degrees of abdominal cramping and diarrhea, can also cause hemolytic uremic syndrome (HUS), an extremely painful disease which sends toxins coursing throughout the body and destroys the blood's ability to clot. HUS, now the leading cause of kidney failure in children in the United States, kills between 5 and 10 percent of its victims and leaves many others disabled.

After weeks in the hospital, Damion was malnourished from eating nothing by mouth, but otherwise seemed at last on the road to recovery.

"And then what comes next?" says Mary. "So we're all celebrating that our child finally made it, and we gave him something to drink. He took a few sips and then he collapsed. He looked at us in total agony, then passed out. What we had watched was that he was perforating his intestines. It was the first time they were challenged, and they just couldn't handle it. They just dissolved.

"So now his intestines are emptying out into his abdominal cavity. He's rushed into emergency surgery. Three-thirty in the morning, and the doctor comes back from unraveling our son's intestinal tract inch by inch to find the holes, and tells us that he thinks he found them all and sutured them." Nevertheless, the resulting infection required two more surgeries.

It took Damion a year to get back on his feet, figuratively and literally. He had to undergo extensive rehabilitation to learn how to stand and walk again. All told, he'd suffered a series of mini-strokes, had seven surgeries, received more than a hundred units of blood, and lost one-fourth of his body weight and thirty percent of his lungs' function.

※　※　※

E. coli 0157:H7, a once-rare bacterium that wasn't even identified until 1982, has since left a trail of sickness and death across the United States. Pathogens like E. coli and salmonella, which live in the intestinal tracts of livestock and poultry, contaminate meat during sloppy high-speed slaughter and processing operations.

"This disease is so destructive and ugly," Mary said. "And then when you find out what causes it—filth in the country's slaughterhouses in the 1990s. I got so furious about it I had to do something."

What Mary did was to meet with the parents of other victims from around the country. Together they established a food safety group called Safe Tables Our Priority (STOP).

When Mary told me she hoped we could get together when she and several other members of her group came to Washington to go to a Senate symposium on meat inspection, I decided to attend as well. In the meantime, I returned to my immediate concern, the Walker investigation.

☙　☙　☙

There was enough corroborative evidence now to make me believe Walker's claims. But all of the people I'd questioned were USDA employees, and now they had to be worried about their jobs because they'd spoken with me.

I went back to Kaplan Industries in Florida.

There were about 260 employees at Kaplan. The majority of them were of Mexican descent. I knew that there were a few Spanish-speaking communities about twenty-five miles south of Kaplan. I got in my car and headed south.

Bowling Green, a half-hour drive from Bartow, looked like a ghost town. The roads were mainly dirt, the houses seemed unlived-in. Most small-town post offices are happy to help with local information, but the one in Bowling Green wasn't willing to give me the names of any Kaplan workers. I headed a few miles down the road to Wauchula, a town of about three thousand. Surrounded by orange and grapefruit groves, Wauchula's resident population swells with Mexican migrant workers who come to the area to pick fruit.

The employment office in Wauchula would not give me names of people they had placed at Kaplan. I tried chatting up the job hunters there but none of them spoke English. I checked out the local bars and cafés, and run-down trailer parks. Same story—no Kaplan workers.

In a convenience store where I stopped to buy cough syrup for my sore throat, I asked the clerk if she knew any Kaplan workers. Lots, she said—the store cashed their paychecks. She didn't know any names, but pointed me in the direction of a house where she thought some of them lived. On the way over, I stopped a nice-looking young man and asked if he spoke English. He did and for ten dollars, he agreed to act as my translator.

As I walked across the lawn of the run-down wooden house, the screen door flew open and a stocky, gray-haired woman stepped out onto the porch. A dog yapped inside.

"What do you want?" the woman demanded.

I smiled and spoke softly. I explained that I was interested in improving the conditions at Kaplan, and that I had heard she had some plant employees living there.

Gertrude Schneider had a one-bedroom cabin in her backyard in which twelve Mexican workers lived. These bare facts suggest a typical immigrant-laborer exploitation scene, but Gertrude herself did not.

"I love my boys," she said. "I take care of them best I can. They're my life."

She agreed to vouch for me with her "boys" when they came home that night. I made an appointment to meet my translator later, went to find something to eat, then sat in my car in the dark parking lot of an abandoned store to wait.

* * *

Most of Gertrude's tenants seemed to be in their early twenties, but their ages and immigration statuses were not of concern to me. Gertrude doted on them and they obviously returned her affection. They all worked hard and sent their meager wages back to their families in Mexico.

While most of these men picked grapefruit in local groves, two had recently worked at Kaplan. Stationed near the blood pit, they'd toiled in constant fear for their lives. Juan Sanchez had quit after only a few days on the job, sure that he'd be crushed by a falling cow. José Alvaro, who had worked there for several months, described what it was like to work in the plant.

Through the interpreter Alvaro said, "My job was to wash the heads. I could see just about everything from where I worked." This included conscious cows thrashing while hanging from the rail, head-skinners cutting spinal cords to stop the kicking, and a line speed too fast for the men to keep up.

Gertrude said nothing while Alvaro spoke, and I was hardly aware of her presence. Later, when I listened to the tape, her gasps of horror came through audibly.

Alvaro said that even after workers were grazed by falling cattle, they were afraid to speak up. I asked him why. He snapped his fingers and pointed over his shoulder with a thumb, hitchhiker style.

"Fired. Right away. On the spot," my translator told me. "Or moved to a different, much worse job, to get them to quit."

* * *

For the affidavits, I was going to need a Spanish-speaking notary public. Gertrude knew one in Bowling Green. Anna Pedrosa worked for a car dealership as well as being a notary. She was petite, spirited, and very helpful once she learned what I was doing. Her brother had worked at Kaplan and she'd heard the stories.

Anna gave me directions to a trailer on the outskirts of town where her brother Hector lived. We sat outside on the grass, a rooster crowing in the distance every few minutes. Hector's thick accent didn't prevent him from painting a vivid picture for me.

"There's too many cows there, and the man killing them, he doesn't have enough time to do it. They hang them up anyway, kicking real hard."

"How many?" I asked.

"Sixty to seventy cattle a day were kicking after they were hung up."

"Some people say that when they kick, it's just muscle reaction," I said.

"Well, maybe that's true. But sometimes they start yelling, 'Moo!' They're hanging down and still yelling moo. They pick up their heads, and their eyes look around. Sometimes they fall down and they try to stand up again. When the cow's hanging down from the rail and is still yelling, uh—"

"Mooing?" I asked.

"Yeah. Mooing. Right. I think they are still alive when they do that. Everybody could tell those cows were alive."

❋   ❋   ❋

Perhaps it was luck or just good old-fashioned detective work that led me to a low-income housing project in Bowling Green. The apartment was dark—there was no answer to my knocking. I hung around until dusk, when I saw a couple climbing out of a car with two small children and their arms full of grocery bags. I followed them into their apartment while introducing myself.

Albert Cabrera, a tall, slim man of about twenty with dark curly hair and huge brown eyes, invited me to sit down. A small electric fan nudged the hot, humid evening air around the room. A cockroach scurried by. I turned on my tape recorder.

"In the morning the big holdup was the calves," he said. "To get done with them faster, we'd put eight or nine of them in the knocking box at a time. As soon as they start going in, you start shooting, the calves are jumping, they're all piling up on top of each other. You don't know which ones got shot and which ones didn't get shot at all, and you forget to do the bottom ones. They're hung anyway, and down the line they go, wriggling and yelling. The baby ones—two, three weeks old—I felt bad killing them so I just let them walk past.

"But it wasn't just the calves that went through conscious. It was a serious problem with the cows, and the bulls have even harder skulls. A lot I had to hit three or five times, ten times before they'd go down. There were plenty of times you'd have to make a big hole in their head, and still they'd be alive.

"I remember one bull with really long horns. I knocked it twice," he said. "Some solid white stuff came out—brains, I guess—and it went down, its face all bloody. I rolled it into the shackling area. That bull must have felt the shackle going on its leg, it got up like nothing ever happened to it, it didn't even wobble, and took off out the back door, started running down Route 17 and just wouldn't stop. They went out and shot it with a rifle, dragged it back with the tractor.

"See, they got a little poster that shows you a little X on its head," Cabrera explained. "And that's where you're supposed to hit them—right there on the center of the X."

"And that's what you tried to do?" I asked.

"That's what I *did* do. But they were always complaining I wasn't doing my job."

"What about the USDA people?" I asked.

"They used to watch the animals stand up after I knocked them. They'd complain but they never did anything about it," he said. "Never. The USDA vet, Dr. Tecsan, would stand there to see how many live ones were going in. I'd be shooting every one five, six times. She'd yell at me but she'd never stop the line. They don't slow that line down for nothing or nobody."

At the end of our interview I checked a few basic facts with him—names, dates—and found he'd knocked at Kaplan some of the same days Walker had drawn blood there. Then I left Albert Cabrera and drove back to my motel. I was encouraged to have located the knocker—the man who could best corroborate Walker's claims.

*　*　*

Armed with accounts from USDA and Kaplan employees, I wanted to obtain a statement from a plant supervisor. One Kaplan foreman gave me more confirmation but, worried about possible reprisals, he refused to go on record. Instead, he gave me another name: Billy Corbet.

I met Corbet—a tall, handsome, transplanted New Englander with brown hair and a mustache—at home with his wife and kids on a pleasant tree-lined street a few miles from the Kaplan plant. He'd worked as a Kaplan supervisor for six years before quitting a few months earlier.

"Kaplan's is a sweatshop," Corbet told me. "The place is falling apart. They buy whatever animals they can. Old, worn-out cattle like spent dairy cows. A lot of them die in the trucks or the holding pens before slaughter." he said.

"What happens to the ones who can't walk off the trucks?" I asked.

"You'd drive an old, worn-out tractor with a bucket up to the truck. The bucket had a chain attached to it. You'd take the chain and fasten it around one of the animal's legs. By lifting the tractor's bucket you'd take up the chain's slack and lift the animal. The animal would be hanging upside down by its leg, and you'd drive it over to a pasture.

"Once you got the downers [animals unable to stand or walk] in the pasture, you were supposed to try to get them back on their feet by putting your fingers in the animal's nose and pulling like crazy. Even when you got a cow to its feet, it always seemed like whenever you checked on it, like a half-hour later, it had flopped over on its side.

"On bad days you'd have over thirty downers," he continued. "A lot of them had fevers, some as high as a hundred and six. Dr. Tecsan wouldn't let us kill those animals until their fevers dropped below a hundred and five." (Federal regulations state that cattle cannot be slaughtered for human consumption if they have a fever over a hundred and five—their normal temperature being 101°.)

"She'd come down and take their temperatures but never

did anything to help them. They'd lie out in that hot sun, maybe for three days, before they died or Dr. Tecsan told us we could shoot them. These animals only got food or water if they could drag themselves up to the hay or water troughs.*

"A lot of times even the healthy ones would go without food or water for a day or two. You might or might not put food out for them, and sometimes they'd be left that way all weekend. The water troughs in the holding pens break down a lot, and it would be months before maintenance would fix them. Animals are left baking in the sun without water. That's why so many of them collapse.

"Another thing—the USDA is supposed to check the animals and mark on the ticket if any cattle are suspect. I've seen inspectors walk in and sign half a day's worth of tickets without even looking at the animals, then go off and have a cup of coffee."

"How do they move the ones that are still on their feet?" I asked.

"You can get frustrated when you're trying to move cattle along," he replied. "Sometimes you have to prod them a lot. But some of the drivers like to burn the hell out of them. The five or six hotshots [electric prods] by the lead-up chutes are hooked directly to a 110-volt outlet. Run them along the floor's metal grates and they spit sparks like a welding machine. Some drivers would beat cattle with hotshots until they were so wild and panicky you couldn't do a thing with

---

*Federal regulations prohibit the dragging of conscious animals and require that disabled animals be placed in covered pens. They also stipulate that animals in holding pens have access to water at all times, and access to food if held over 24 hours.

them, right up into the knocking box, then they'd just stand there and laugh." (Federal law prohibits the excessive use of electric prods and states that they must be used at the lowest possible voltage, not to exceed 50 volts.)

"Didn't anyone ever say anything?"

"[Corporation President] Don Kaplan had an arrangement," Corbet said. "If an employee complained, a supervisor would put him on a much harder job—usually in the hide room, where they'd have to take hides off the rail, spread them out, and put salt on them. It's a terrible job. Instead of firing someone who complains, he'd put them down there and they'd quit pretty quick."

*   *   *

I headed back to Washington. A few days later, Timothy Walker called me with some bad news: The USDA had fired him for speaking to me.

4

"Mommy, Am I Going to Die?"

Are you brave enough to admit that the one natural reservoir of E. coli 0157:H7 has been proven to be the intestinal tract of cattle? That the avenue of infection is feces splattered on our meat? That the disease which was extremely rare only a decade ago has now become the leading cause of kidney failure in U.S. children? That all this suffering is in direct correlation to the deregulatory programs of the last two administrations?
—Mary Heersink, founder, Safe Tables Our Priority,
to USDA officials at a hearing on meat inspection,
June 1993

Like most government workers, Timothy Walker had to work for the USDA for one year before being granted the job secu-

49

rity of a permanent federal employee. He had been employed by the USDA for 363 days, just two days shy of his permanent appointment, when the USDA fired him for speaking to me.

I called in GAP's promise to represent Walker, faxed Freedom of Information Act requests to the USDA, and started phoning and visiting my other Washington contacts.

✻   ✻   ✻

Mary Heersink—whose son, Damion, had nearly died after eating a morsel of tainted hamburger—had a pretty face, long blonde hair, and a quiet way of speaking that made you feel you were talking with an old friend. When I met her at the Senate symposium, she was accompanied by a group of a dozen or so other parents whose children had been poisoned by contaminated meat. Some of them had their children with them. Others did not—theirs had not survived. Instead, these parents brought along framed photographs of their children for display at the symposium. Once the symposium convened, they told their stories into a microphone.

Ten-year-old Brianne Kiner was the first to take the floor. She told us she'd gotten sick after eating a tainted and under-cooked hamburger at a fast-food restaurant. Brianne only spoke for a minute, but even that seemed to exhaust her.

Brianne's mother, Suzanne Kiner, followed her daughter's presentation with a story of her own.

> My daughter Brianne lay in a hospital bed for one hundred sixty-seven days. For fifty-five of those days she was dying.
> Our story begins with a tainted hamburger she ate in early January. Within a few days, Bri had a fever of 103.8°

and abdominal cramps. She turned pale and became very quiet. That night we had to make a frantic visit to our pediatrician because Bri was bleeding from her rectum.

Later, I carried my daughter to the rest room to collect a urine sample. When I brought the cup up it was filled with blood that spilled onto my hand. When Brianne asked, "What is it Mommy? I told her it was the raspberry Popsicle she'd sucked on 6 hours earlier. . . . My nine-year-old child with the dancing brown eyes and long matching brown hair had just begun a five-and-a-half-month battle.

The pain during her first eighty hours in the hospital was horrific. The intense abdominal cramping continued every ten to twelve minutes. Her intestines swelled to three times their normal size.

She fell into a deep coma that lasted forty days. All of her body organs swelled. Her breathing accelerated to a hundred breaths per minute so she was placed on a ventilator.

When the doctors told us Brianne had only an hour to live, we began a communion to celebrate her life. The doctors rushed her into emergency surgery to remove her colon even though they still gave her little chance of survival. Miraculously, Brianne survived that night.

After Brianne's second emergency surgery, surgeons left her open from her sternum to her pubic area to allow her swollen organs room to expand and prevent them from ripping her skin. We were told Brianne had no chance of surviving. At one point her heart stopped beating, but the doctor revived her. Her heart was so swollen it was like a sponge. It bled from every pore.

The toxins shut down Bri's liver and pancreas. Several times her skin turned black for weeks. An insulin pump was started. She had a brain swell that the neurologists could not treat with medication. EEGs revealed thousands of grand-mal seizures, which had caused blood clots in her eyes.

Then the neurologists told us that Brianne was essentially brain dead. She had a five percent chance of surviving as a vegetable, a ninety-five percent chance of dying.

The Brianne who traveled to Washington to testify before Congress had beaten the odds, but she had also paid a high price. She had heart disease, brain damage, diabetes, and seriously scarred lungs. She had only one-third of her liver, she'd been on dialysis for months, and she'd had pneumonia twice. Her mother told the symposium that the muscles throughout her body had atrophied, necessitating extensive physical and occupational therapy.

Brianne still has a "micky button" attached to her stomach from the surface of her skin. A special formula is fed to her every night by a feeding pump attached to her "button" while she sleeps. . . . HUS [hemolytic uremic syndrome] caused the entire lining of her stomach to be burned. It is solid scar tissue. Because of this, she can only eat seven bites at each meal during the day.

Once a talkative child, Brianne no longer had much to say. She was so weak she could attend her fourth-grade class for only one hour every other school day.

※   ※   ※

The Dolans' two daughters—Aundrea, three, and Mary, four—both became violently sick within days of eating hamburgers at a Seattle fast-food restaurant. They were taken to the hospital. Their mother, Dorothy Dolan, a nurse, told the story:

> My husband and I spent the next two days carrying our daughters to the bathroom, listening to the moans and groans during the nights and the screams during the day. While the bloody diarrhea continued and Mary kept saying "Mommy please take the pain away," both she and Aundrea were slipping further and further into this terrible illness. On January 12th Mary woke up with a bloody nose and blood in her urine. While on the toilet, she looked up at me with her big blue eyes and asked, "Mommy, am I going to die?"
>
> My worst fears were coming true. The doctors informed me that Mary had developed HUS and was going downhill. They looked at Aundrea and said that she was following the same course. The next morning Aundrea, too, had blood in her urine and a bloody nose. . . .
>
> Next, Mary was screaming that her head hurt. We cuddled next to her and hugged her tight, but the screams kept coming. "MAMA! MAMA!" I called her name and held her tight, but she couldn't focus her eyes at me, they stared fixated off to the left. She kept calling for me as if she didn't know I was holding her.
>
> My husband ran to get the nurse and the doctor. While we were waiting for what seemed like hours, Mary was getting worse. Her mouth was closing, her left side wasn't moving, and her cries for help were more and more slurred. . . .

A CAT-scan led to a diagnosis: Mary had suffered a stroke.

> The doctors told us Mary's prognosis was poor. They said the toxin could continue to spread to her other organs, the

liver, pancreas, lungs, and heart, her teeth could even fall out. She could die.

We waited every four to six hours for her lab results. In the meantime, we got to hold her with all her lines attached. It was like holding a sack of potatoes, she was so limp, had no body tone. Her feet were swollen, the right side of her face was swollen because her kidneys weren't working well. She tried to sit up but had no strength and would just collapse back down.

Mary was moved to a regular room the same day Aundrea was discharged. We had to get Mary to eat, teach her to sit up and hold her head up, to walk, to use the bathroom again. She got physical therapy, speech therapy, occupational therapy. The doctors told us we could take her home and continue therapy on an outpatient basis.

The day finally came when Mary could go home. She was weak. She couldn't take two steps without falling. Her body was skin and bones with a protruding abdomen. She looked as if she had been through the battle of her life—which, of course, she had.

*   *   *

"No words can truly convey what this hideous disease did to our three-year-old daughter," said Robert Galler, the next parent to speak. "It literally took over Lois Joy's life. During her eighteen days in the hospital, she had sixteen blood transfusions, fourteen dialysis treatments, her lungs had to be tapped because they filled with fluid, she had to be put on a respirator, she lost sight in her right eye, her brain was bleeding, she had a stroke. We watched helpless as our daughter died right before our eyes."

While children suffering from HUS exhibit specific symptoms, few doctors know to test for the bacteria. Little Lois Joy Galler was treated for an ear infection for days before she was hospitalized.

       ❁   ❁   ❁

Roni Rudolph, from San Diego, described her six-year-old Lauren's "golden red silky hair, sparkling brown eyes and a smile that would light up your heart." A week before Christmas, Lauren's dad had taken her and her brother to a fast-food restaurant to celebrate the good grades they'd gotten at school that week. A few days later, Lauren had bloody diarrhea and wrenching stomach pain.

During a break Mary Heersink told me, "When I and all these other parents say bloody diarrhea, we're not talking about just a little blood. It's a hemorrhage. Every ten minutes it looks like someone poured a quart of clotted blood down the toilet."

Lauren Rudolph's parents rushed her to the hospital. Despite the fact she couldn't walk, the doctor diagnosed her as having a flu and sent her home. On Christmas Eve she was finally admitted to the hospital.

"Christmas morning we found her worsening, the pain still increasing," her mother said. "She was in diapers, an IV in her wrist, and large quantities of painkillers weren't working. We brought her presents to the hospital. She smiled at us but could not open them, she felt so bad."

That evening, after reading Lauren Christmas stories, the Rudolphs went home.

"I went upstairs to just sit for a few minutes in Lauren's

room," Mrs. Rudolph said. "I found a note Lauren had left Santa. It said, 'Dear Santa, I don't feel so good. Please make me well for Christmas. Love, Lauren.'"

The Rudolphs returned to the hospital the next morning. Their daughter had taken a turn for the worse. "She'd been telling her father, 'I'm going to die! I'm going to die!' I took her hand and told her she was going to be okay. An hour and a half later Lauren had a massive heart attack—at the age of six."

Two days later, a second heart attack took her life.

5

The Fall Guy

USDA regional supervisors met privately to discuss the Walker case. Then they asked Walker's immediate boss to write a letter criticizing his performance. She refused, saying that Walker had been a model USDA employee and that his concerns about Kaplan were justified. In a previous job-performance evaluation, she had rated Walker "fully successful" or "exceeds fully successful" in all his duties, and praised him for his "out of the ordinary" concern for animals and workers at Kaplan.

But now, after speaking with me, Walker was facing retaliation. USDA Southeast Regional Director Dr. Lloyd D. Konyha sent Walker a three-page letter. "I have received documentation that demonstrates to me that you have failed to fully demonstrate your qualifications for continued employment. I have determined that your overall conduct is nonacceptable and that your continued employment is not in the best interest of Federal Service."

Konyha then made a tactical blunder by openly committing the following to writing: "Your recent decision to direct your criticisms outside the Agency to a public humane group has resulted in our working relationships with the Kaplan management to have been irreparably damaged for the foreseeable future." Further, he said, the "fragile relationship" between the USDA and the plant was "almost destroyed by your decision to take your criticisms to the public rather than through the Agency itself."

In firing Walker for trying to get action from outside the USDA, Dr. Konyha was breaking the federal Whistleblower Protection Act—and he was documenting his malfeasance with his own letter.

In closing, Konyha commented, "For the reasons cited above, I am convinced that your general traits are incompatible with the duties related to your position. It is my decision that to continue your employment beyond the probationary period would impede the efficiency of government service."

PART TWO

THE STICKERS' CONFESSIONS

6

The Man with the Scar

As for me, I was working like mad transcribing the interviews I'd taped and turning them into affidavits. This was all very powerful, but I was concerned that the meat industry might try to explain Kaplan away as a backwater anachronism. I suspected, however, that Kaplan was representative of slaughterhouses across the country. So I decided to broaden my investigation's scope and started researching the entire U.S. meat industry.

I obtained statistics from various government sources. The slaughter figures were staggering. One hundred and one million pigs are slaughtered each year in the United States. Thirty-seven million cattle and calves. More than four million horses, goats, and sheep. And over eight *billion* chickens and turkeys. In all, annually in the United States farmers produce 65 billion pounds of cattle and pigs and beef, 46 billion pounds of chickens and turkeys, and 80 billion eggs.

Lax enforcement of antitrust laws during the Reagan and Bush administrations, I learned, had allowed a consolidation of meatpacking power to levels higher than at any time in history, and a corresponding deregulation of slaughterhouse procedures. According to the USDA, between 1984 and 1994, a few large, high-speed slaughter operations had driven roughly 2,000 small to mid-sized packers out of business—one-third of all packers in the United States. They also reduced the workforce while cranking up the killing speeds. Fewer employees were slaughtering more animals, and, according to the United Food and Commercial Workers International Union, which represents thousands of slaughterhouse employees, the worker turnover rate in high-speed plants approached 100 percent per year.*

☙   ☙   ☙

I glanced through the pile of complaints on my desk that had gathered as I worked on my slaughterhouse case. A guy in North Carolina strangled a hundred puppies for fun; a New Yorker collected two hundred homeless pets and then starved them to death. Just when I thought I'd seen it all, some new way to torture animals would land in my in-box.

---

*According to the USDA, in 1980, it took the country's 50 largest beef packing companies and 103 individual plants to slaughter three-quarters of the nation's cattle. By 1992, *three* firms were already slaughtering that percentage of animals in 29 plants. In 1996 more than 40 percent of the nation's cattle were killed in a mere 11 plants that slaughter more than one million animals each year. Similarly, more than 40 percent of the nation's hogs were killed in 10 plants.

I thumbed through *Animal's Voice,* an animal protection magazine I found buried among the complaints and tossed it aside. Then something I'd flipped past registered and I opened it up again. It was an article about one of the huge, high-speed meat packers I'd just been researching. And the main difference between the abuses described there and those at Kaplan was that the animals depicted were not cattle, but hogs—and they were reportedly being immersed in the plant's scalding tank and boiled alive.

According to the story, a union official at the John Morrell & Company slaughterhouse in Sioux City, Iowa, claimed that hogs at that plant were not being properly stunned and were still fully conscious as they were submerged in the plant's scalding tank. "What the public sees is fancy labels," said the official who'd had twenty-four years' experience in the packing industry. "But those of us inside the walls can tell the truth about what the vast majority have never seen—living hell in John Morrell's slaughterhouse." With the article appeared a full-page photo of the plant's night-shift sticker slitting a hog's throat.

I contacted the magazine for more information, threw some clothes and my paperback copy of *The Jungle* into a suitcase, and headed for the airport.

❋   ❋   ❋

Mike Huntsinger, the union official quoted in the magazine, was a burly man with a direct manner. He told me that while John Morrell & Company had the capacity to slaughter seventy-five thousand hogs a week at the breakneck speed of one hog every four seconds, line speed was only part of the problem. Hogs were stunned electrically rather than mechanically; electrodes

Hog Slaughter

... shackled and hoisted ▲

... ▲ Hog is shocked
with electrical "stunner"

Hogs are driven
to restrainer ...
▶

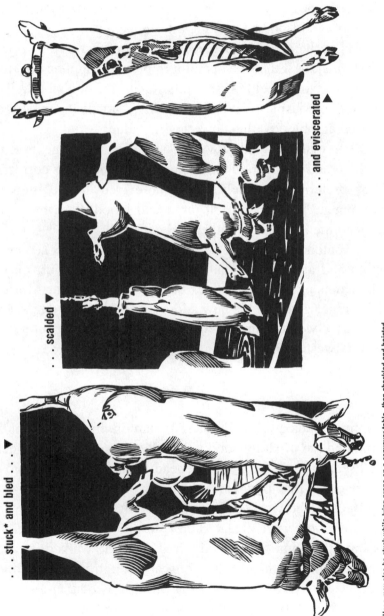

. . . stuck* and bled . . . . ▶

. . . scalded ▶

. . . and eviscerated ▲

*Hogs may also be stuck while lying prone on a conveyor table, then shackled and hoisted.

held to the hog's head and back sent a three-second jolt of current through its body, knocking the animal out.

But if the animal was excessively prodded on its way to the stunner, or if the stun operator improperly applied the electrodes, the jolt would burst capillaries in the hog's back. The result—"bloodsplash" or "blown loins"—made the meat look bruised and bloody, thus lowering its value.

Plant managers didn't want to slow down the line, ease up on the prodding, or train the stunners to do their jobs correctly. They preferred to simply lower the current to the stunning equipment. The weaker jolt prevented bloodsplash but often stunned the hogs only momentarily, if at all.

I wanted to talk to the sticker, the man on the scene whose photo had appeared in the magazine. He'd been hurt on the job, Huntsinger told me, and no longer worked at Morrell. Huntsinger gave me his new address and I headed out. A ten-hour drive would bring me to a quiet mobile home community in southwestern Kansas.

*   *   *

Tommy Vladak, a sandy-haired man in his mid-twenties, reminded me of Hollywood's Brad Pitt—except for the puckered scar that ran from his forehead, across his eye and nose, and over his lips to his jaw.

Because he worked the evening shift at his new job, my first interview with Vladak didn't start until almost midnight. Despite the hour, he seemed wired when he walked into my motel room. His hand felt strong and rough when he shook mine. He sat down, declined my offer of a soda, and said he was ready to talk. I turned on my tape recorder.

Vladak seemed proud of his nine years' experience in the packing industry. Originally from Texas, Vladak and his wife and kids had moved to Sioux City to be closer to his in-laws.

"What was it like, being a sticker at Morrell?" I asked.

"Dangerous," Vladak said. "I was kicked, bitten, stabbed in the forearm, had a tooth knocked out, an eardrum punctured, and finally got my face slashed. And that was *after* I'd complained about live hogs to almost every level of management, and had shut the chain off a bunch of times trying to deal with the problem.

"I was a good sticker. I could do the job at any chain speed. At Morrell's I was sticking about nine hundred hogs an hour, which wouldn't be that hard if they were stunned right. But when most of them are fully conscious, kicking and biting at you, it's like . . ."

He looked around the room, as if searching for a comparison.

"I used to make a joke when I was down there," he said. "I'd say them motherfuckers who do kickboxing, karate, tae kwon do, they got nothing on me. I felt like I could've gone ten rounds with Mike Tyson and whooped his ass.

"When I first started the job, I ate speed just to keep up with all the live hogs. The third period was the roughest because the supervisors would crank up the chain speed to get their quota out. They'd say, 'Let's rock and roll!' You'd look at the clock and figure out how many hogs you had left to kill. When it was finally over, you'd go home and just die."

He was sitting with his feet flat on the shag carpet, his hands curled around the arms of the chair, his eyes dark and hard, telling me how good he was at a job that had nearly killed him.

"Tell me about the kill line," I said. "From the top."

"It begins at the lead-up chutes when the hogs are brought in from the yards. Two or three drivers chase the hogs up. They prod them a lot because the hogs don't want to go. When hogs smell blood, they don't want to go.

"I've seen hogs beaten, whipped, kicked in the head to get them up to the restrainer.* One night I saw a driver get so angry at a hog he broke its back with a piece of board. I've seen hog drivers take their prod and shove it up the hog's ass to get them to move. I didn't appreciate that because it made the hogs twice as wild by the time they got to me."

"Don't they get stunned before they go to the sticker?" I asked.

"Management was constantly complaining to us about blown loins," he replied. "They claimed that when the stunner voltage was set too high it tore up the meat. The supervisors always wanted it on low stun no matter what size hogs we were stunning. Then when you got big sows and boars in the restrainer, the stunner wouldn't work at all.

"I yelled so much about having to stick live hogs, the stun operator would double-stun them. I'd watch him hitting them two and three times, and still they'd come through conscious.

"I've seen hogs stunned up to twelve times. Like, a big boar would come through, they'd hit him with the stunner, he'd look up at them, go RRRAAA! Hit him again, the son of a bitch wouldn't go, wouldn't go. It's amazing the willpower these animals have.

---

*The restrainer is comprised of two angled conveyor belts that support the hogs by their sides. The pigs are prodded into the restrainer single file, then, with their legs dangling beneath them, transported up to the stun operator.

"One night I asked somebody on the kill floor how many loins we'd blown out that night. Two or three. How come they lowered the stunner voltage for just two or three out of thousands? Two or three's still too many, they said."

"What about the stun operators?" I asked. "Couldn't they deal with the blown-loin problem some other way?"

"There was basic incompetence among the stun operators," Vladak said. "One guy would set the stunner on the hog's back, then instead of holding the wand down for the three-second stun, he'd let it go and watch it ride up the hog's back and shock the hog. He enjoyed watching the hog jump in the air when it was shocked. He liked to watch them flip up. He did this a lot until one time the hog jumped up and the wand fell off and zapped him. Then he decided he'd better stop doing it."

Vladak explained that, adequately stunned or not, the hogs then slid down onto a conveyor table where a shackler wrapped a shackle around one of the hind legs and hoisted the animal up onto the moving chain. Because improperly stunned hogs could jump off the shackling table, a pen was built below it.

"The catch pen is only about sixteen square feet," Vladak said. "There are never supposed to be more than two hogs down in the catch pen at any time, but I've seen as many as fourteen. Once there are two, the shackler's supposed to shut the chain off, stun the hog with the little portable knocking gun, and hang the hog back on the main chain. After the sticker sticks it, the chain is supposed to be started up again.

"That may be policy," he said, "but that isn't the way things are done at Morrell's. When hogs end up in the catch pen alive, the shackler beats them over the head with a lead pipe a couple of times—until they're dazed so he can get a chain around the hog's leg—and then he hoists it up. By then they may have come back to life and be squealing their heads off. If there are a lot of hogs in the catch pen, the shackler doesn't have the time to use the hand stunner or pipe them. He'd hook them up, hang them alive, and I was expected to stick them.

"A lot of times hogs would jump off the shackling table and land in my little area. They'd been shocked, so they were vicious. They would be biting at anybody or anything that came near them. They'd come after my ass in my little area. Hey, man, I'm not going to stand there and get bit.

"The foreman would be yelling at me, 'Stick that hog before it gets away!' So I'd grab it by the front leg, roll it over on its back and stick it [in the neck], then just get out of there. 'Cause these hogs would spring back up after you stuck them. They would run around in a circle for about five minutes, just bleeding, trying to hold back everything they had. If it was me or the hog, man, it was the hog.

"One night I had a boar come through live—about a five-hundred pounder—and I was about to stick it. It was hanging there upside down and it literally picked itself up [tried to right itself] and looked me right in the face. I grabbed it by its ear and it jerked away. When it came back, its tusk went through my no-cut glove and ripped my finger wide open. I turned around and stuck it. Then I shoved the water hose up its nose to drown it. I was so pissed.

"It got to the point where I was ducking and swerving and dipping so much I referred to my job as dancing. I'd stick the hogs, then as soon as I pulled that knife out, I'd spin them so they wouldn't [squirm and] kick blood in my face. There were nights I looked like I'd been through a bloodbath.

"One night, the night-shift manager was giving a tour to

some Japanese customers. They pass by me and I say, 'Hey Rod, look at this!' I stick a hog and jump back. The hog starts spinning around on the shackle and squealing, splatters some of the customers with blood.

" 'You don't have no goddamn right doing that!' he said. 'Like hell I don't,' I said. 'I'm just doing my job. I told you about the problem two weeks ago. What are you doing about it? You haven't done a goddamn thing. I figured I'd just show it to you personally.' He had blood all over him. The Japanese guys weren't too happy either."

"So the managers knew all about the stunning problem," I said. "Did they ever do anything about it?"

"They'd say, 'That's just muscle reaction, nerves. It's not alive.' I'd say, 'Then why's the damn hog trying to *bite* me? Just how stupid do you think I am?'

"It got to the point where if I had a live hog come at me and I had time, I'd take a lead pipe and beat it over the head until it was knocked out enough for me to stick it. When the supervisor would complain about cracked skulls I'd say, 'Look, I'm just trying to keep my own skull from being busted.' "

"What happens after you stick them?" I asked.

"After they left me, the hogs would go up a hundred-foot ramp to a tank where they're dunked in 140° water [a standard procedure in pork processing]. That's to scald their hair off," he explained. "Water any hotter than that would take the meat right off the bones. You stick a live hog, it tightens up the muscles around that slit and holds the blood in. There's no way these animals can bleed out in the few minutes it takes to get up the ramp. By the time they hit the scalding tank, they're still fully conscious and squealing. Happens all the time.

"One night I was down there and a hog got out of the chutes," he continued. "Son of a bitch took off up the ramp and jumped right into the scald tank. The utility man caught it by the back leg, jerked it out, and held on to that hog. Another guy comes running down, 'Gimme your knife! Gimme your knife!' He went up there and stuck it. That hog had its head, front legs, and half its body in the scald tank, and when the utility man jerked it out, that thing was just thrashing like hell."

He lit a cigarette, inhaled deeply, let the smoke out slowly.

"I got suspended once for missing three hogs," Vladak said. "I'd been working since three that afternoon, and that night there were so many live hogs on the chain I just wasn't able to stick them all. Rod Welles suspended me indefinitely. 'You go home and think about why you cost us X dollars tonight,' he said.

"I was sitting there burning, ready to blow up. I said, cool down, don't blow it now. I asked for union representation but was told I didn't need any.

"The next day Mike Huntsinger from the union and I go to a meeting with Paul Harris, the assistant personnel director. Harris says, 'If you've got a live hog, just shut the goddamned chain off and stick the hog. When a hog doesn't get stuck, it doesn't bleed before going into the scalding tank. When it comes out of the scalding tank and gets opened up, the meat inspector condemns the hog and John Morrell loses a couple hundred dollars.'

"Then the plant superintendent comes in and tells me that whenever I see a live hog, I should 'just shut the chain off and stick the hog. If you're in doubt at any time, just shut the chain off and stick the hog. The main thing is, don't miss any fucking hogs!' That wasn't the first time somebody at Morrell told me to stick live hogs, and it sure wasn't the last. And I did it.

"Huntsinger told Paul Harris I should be paid for the hours I missed the night before. Harris tells him I won't be paid, and that I'm lucky not to be fired."

From time to time Vladak would touch his scar, trace it partway with a finger.

"How'd you cut your face?" I asked.

Again he touched the scar. "One night I went to stick a hog and it was alive so I let it go. Figured I'd catch it later after it calmed down a little," he explained. "So I go to stick the next hog, bend down and put my arm on its belly, and suddenly the first one's front leg catches my arm. I didn't think to drop my knife, and when I hit my face, it was just like I stuck another hog. I was wearing a white shirt, suddenly it's a red shirt, and my apron's completely bloody.

"The nurse starts wrapping gauze around my face, and about four boxes of gauze later, another worker comes in and tells her he's called an ambulance. She says, 'Get over here and put pressure on his face, we can't stop the bleeding. He hit an artery in his face.'

"The knife cut across my mouth and nose, up the left side of my face, under my eye, and through my eyelid. It took four hours of surgery and a hundred twenty-five stitches to close it up," he said. "That night I asked the nurse for a mirror to see my face. She said no, the doctors said I'd go into shock. When I woke up the next day I unhooked the drip from my arm, walked over to the mirror, and looked at my face. That was the first time in two years I'd cried about anything.

"Two guys from Morrell's safety committee told me how

damn lucky I was. That was the last straw. I decided my life was a little bit more important than somebody's damn hogs."

He was staring off into space now, silent. I didn't say a word.

"There was one night I'll never forget as long as I live," he continued. "A little female hog was coming through the chutes. She got away and the supervisor said, 'Stick that bitch!' I grabbed her and flipped her over. She looked up at me. It was like she was saying, 'Yeah, I know it's your job, do it.' That was the first time I ever looked into a live hog's eyes. And I stuck her."

The phone rang, jerking me back to the drab room. Vladak's wife was calling, probably wondering just what kind of an interview was going on in a motel room at two o'clock in the morning. Tommy and I arranged to meet at his place later in the day, and he left.

*　　*　　*

The Vladaks' mobile home was clean and tidy, with children's drawings taped to the walls here and there. Vladak was alone when I arrived. We sat down at the kitchen table next to the one big window. Country music played on the radio.

Last night I'd pretty much gotten all the factual information I'd wanted from him, but I wondered what kind of a person would take on a job like his, and what effect it had had on him.

"You've got to be good," he said. "You can't take just anybody off the street. It's something in your blood. I enjoy the kill, as long as it's done right.

"But when you're standing there night after night, digging that knife into these hogs, and they're fighting you, kicking at you, squealing, trying to bite you—doing whatever they can to try and get away from you—after a while you don't give a shit. You're just putting in your time. And then it gets to a point where you're at a daydream stage. Where you can think about everything else and still do your job. You become emotionally dead.

"And you get just as sadistic as the company itself. When I was sticking down there, I was a sadistic person. By the end of the night everybody would be yelling at everybody else. The stunner would be yelling at the hog drivers to stop prodding the hogs so much. The shackler would be yelling at the stunner to quit sending him live hogs. I'd be yelling at all three of them. Then at the end of the shift we'd hit the local bar and talk about it. Everybody agreed: something's going to happen, somebody's going to get hurt bad. It wasn't a month later I was lying there in the emergency room."

A car pulled up outside. I could see a woman and a child inside.

"The worst part," he continued, "even worse than my accident, was what happened to my family life. I'd come home, my wife would ask me how my night went, and instead of being happy to see her I'd say, 'What the hell do you care?' We'd get into arguments about stupid things. Or else I'd come in so drunk I'd wonder how in the hell I made it home. Then wake up the next morning and start all over again."

We watched a pretty blonde woman climb out of the car. The child, a little girl, ran from the car out of sight around the trailer.

"My wife and I finally separated in early July," Vladak said, "about two weeks before I cut my face. She couldn't take the bitching any more. I'd blow up at the drop of a hat, come home every night and find something to complain about, take my frustrations from work out on my family."

Vladak's wife, Lisa, came in and gave me a warm welcome despite any concerns she may have had about the previous night's late rendezvous.

"I was just telling Gail about my attitude when I worked at Morrell's," Vladak said. "What I was like to live with, and that you finally left me."

"Did you tell her *why* I left you?"

He nodded and looked away. "Somewhat. My attitude."

"No," Lisa said.

"Oh." He was looking at his hands on the table now. "Me slapping her around."

"You were hitting her?" I said.

"Yup."

"He hasn't hit me since then," Lisa said. "Not since I kicked him in the nuts."

He laughed.

"I was a terrible parent, too," he said. "Mean as could be to my kids. They could do the littlest thing wrong, I wouldn't think twice about whooping their asses. Now I still chew their butts, raise my voice, but I'm not as physical with them."

Vladak glanced out the window at his daughter, now playing on a swing. He let out a loud sigh.

"One thing I learned after my accident," Vladak said, "is that nobody's irreplaceable. The minute I left they just hired somebody else. And the minute he gets hurt bad they'll put somebody else down there. And the chain will just keep going. Because people need a job, and they're willing to do anything they can to keep their job. I proved it by sticking live animals.

I did it, I just wanted that job, that weekly paycheck. Today, if somebody gave me a choice of going without a job or working for John Morrell's, I'd go without a job. I'd mow lawns, fix cars. I'd do anything before I'd do that again."

7

Pangs of Conscience

I decided to cross-check Vladak's story by questioning his replacement at Morrell. Steve Jansson was a polite young man with no ax to grind.

"You're talking to someone who loves this job," said Jansson when we first spoke.

Soon I was hearing about the same conscious hogs, worker injuries, and blind-eyed management—recounted this time as the natural perils of a life of adventure. He hadn't been working at Morrell long, but already a hog he was sticking had bitten him badly enough to require medical care.

"The stunners aren't worth shit," he said.

It turned out that the same stun operator who'd sent Vladak to the hospital was now stunning for Jansson.

"This stunner," Jansson said, "he already got one guy

stabbed in the face. Everybody knows he stinks at his job. But when that hog comes at me alive, I don't care where I hit him—whether I hit him high or I hit him low. I just poke a hole in him and get out as fast as I can. That's all that's required of me. I don't care if he bleeds good or not."

*　　*　　*

Ed Van Winkle's name kept popping up in conversations around Morrell's, usually in a tone that let you know you were hearing about a living legend. Since the 1960s, he'd worked just about every kill-floor job at ten different plants. I'd heard stories about him—the most ferocious of the stickers.

We met at the Holiday Inn coffee shop in Sioux City. A husky man in his early forties with bushy, brown hair and a beard, he was polite but distant at first, aloof rather than fierce. As soon as I asked about working in the blood pit he brought up the same thing—conscious, struggling hogs.

"Do you think the problem is a function of the stun operators?" I asked him. "Or the equipment?"

"I think the whole problem is the attitude," he replied. "As long as that chain is running, they don't give a shit what you have to do to get that hog on the line. You got to get a hog on each hook or you got a foreman on your ass."

Van Winkle sounded tired, worn down, too battle-scarred to bother with machismo.

"When I started with Morrell it was a very different company. At some point there was a dramatic switch, caused by greed, in my opinion. Production took precedence over employee welfare. If someone got hurt, you weren't supposed to shut the chain off; you were supposed to drag him off the floor and keep the chain going. The chain became the most important thing. Everything else fell by the wayside.

"In the last few years, conditions at Morrell's have gotten worse and worse. Today, management doesn't care how the hog gets up on that line. Management doesn't care whether the hog is stunned or conscious, or whether the sticker is injured in the process. All Morrell cares about is getting those hogs killed.

"When I first started driving hogs for Morrell back in 1985, we used leather slappers to prod them. But whipping the hogs hard with these slappers left marks on the animals and damaged the meat, so management started issuing hotshots. One touch of that electric prod gets an animal to move, but at Morrell's they were vicious with them. If a hog don't want to go up to the restrainer and you don't have a pipe handy, you shove the prod in his eye. And you hold it in his eye. And that changes his attitude."

The coffee shop smelled of bacon and sausage.

"All the drivers do this?" I asked.

Van Winkle was quiet for a few moments. "This is kind of hard to talk about," he said softly. "You're under all this stress, all this pressure. And it really sounds mean but," he was speaking almost in a whisper, "I've taken prods and stuck them in their eyes. And held them there."*

The waitress brought us coffee and menus. Van Winkle said he didn't need a menu, he'd have an English muffin. I ordered the same.

"What else do the drivers do?" I asked.

---

*Workers know that by creating a "hole in the line"—a momentary lapse in the flow of animals—and causing employees down line to stand idle, they are putting their jobs at risk.

"The preferred method of handling a cripple at Morrell's is to beat him to death with a lead pipe before he gets into the chute. It's called 'piping.' All the drivers use pipes to kill hogs that can't go through the chutes. Or if you get a hog that refuses to go in the chutes and is stopping production, you beat him to death. Then push him off to the side and hang him up later."*

"How often does that happen?" I asked.

"I've beaten eleven to death in one day. I hope that don't sound like bragging, because it's not."

"Don't worry about it," I said. "Just tell me what was happening."

"Hogs get stressed out pretty easy," he continued. "If you prod them too much they have heart attacks. If you get a hog in the chute that's had the shit prodded out of him and has a heart attack or refuses to move, you take a meat hook and hook it into his bunghole [anus]. You try to do this by clipping the hipbone. Then you drag him backwards. You're dragging these hogs alive, and a lot of times the meat hook rips out of the bunghole. I've seen hams—thighs—completely ripped open. I've also seen intestines come out. If the hog collapses near the front of the chute, you shove the meat hook into his cheek and drag him forward."

He took a sip of black coffee.

"What happens when hogs reach the restrainer?" I asked.

"They've been shocked in the ass, poked in the eye, and they're about as hyper as a pig can be. They're climbing on top of each other. They're nuts. The guy working the restrainer has

---

*Humane slaughter regulations prohibit the use of pipes, sharp objects, and other dangerous devices to prod—no less beat to death—slaughter animals.

to try to catch these bouncing hogs with a stunner. They're jumping around, knocking the stunner off, and you're not getting a solid stun."

"Don't the stun operators learn how to deal with that during their training?"

For the first time, Van Winkle smiled. "Training? Someone tells the stun operator, 'You put the stunner on the hog.' End of training. The stunner and shackler rotate jobs, but most of the training's about shackling procedures. Management is more concerned with getting the hog on the line than with getting a good stun. And since the early eighties, foremen at Morrell's have been turning down the stunner voltage, which makes a good stun impossible."

Our muffins came. Van Winkle spread some jam on his and took a bite.

"You'd think management would want a good stun," I said.

"I went to the foremen about it," he replied. "I went to the main foreman. We kept telling them we were slaughtering conscious hogs. We asked them to set the stunner voltage high enough to knock the hogs out. We said we could try this, try that. The main foreman would agree to take care of the problem then just walk away. Five minutes later, when we knew he was in another area, we'd run upstairs to the control room and turn up the voltage. What does management do? Puts a lock on the control-room door."

Van Winkle wasn't as ornery as I'd thought from my first impression. Sorrow shone in his deep-brown eyes when he described what he'd seen—and done.

"When I first started sticking," he continued, "the blood collection tank only had a two-inch pipe to drain out all the blood, so it filled up fast. When the hogs came through the stick pit, their whole heads might be hanging in the blood. If the line was running, the hogs didn't stay submerged for long, but if the chain stopped, they were stuck in the blood. I can remember conscious hogs blowing bubbles in the blood collection tank—it was just sickening.

"Morrell installed a new blood collection system and the tanks didn't fill up as quickly. Still, whenever the pump broke down, hogs would be dragging their heads through the blood.

"Because of the line speed, the sticker only gets one chance to make a good stick hole," he explained, "or the hog bleeds real slow. The sticker doesn't have time to go digging around for arteries. If the hog is conscious and tries to hold onto its blood by constricting its muscles—that's his blood and he's not letting go of it—the blood comes out in a trickle and it takes a long time for him to bleed out.

"Bad-sticks usually don't have a chance to bleed out. They end up drowning in the scalding tank before they ever bleed to death. These hogs get up to the scalding tank, hit the water and start screaming and kicking. Sometimes they thrash so much they kick water out of the tank. Not a lot of water, but it was obvious what was going on because I could hear them screaming. Sooner or later they drown," he said. "There's a rotating arm that pushes them under, no chance for them to get out. I'm not sure if they burn to death before they drown, but it takes them a couple of minutes to stop thrashing. You think management cares about the pain of being drowned or boiled to death?"

"You seemed to care," I said.

"Mistake I made," he said, "was thinking of it as a problem that would be solved if I was just persistent enough, if I just got through to the right person. I'd go to the office, I'd go to

OSHA [Occupational Safety and Health Administration], USDA. I'd say, look, we got live hogs here. Number one, people are getting cut. Number two, it's cruel. No one would take action. I was also the safety representative for the union, and I got lots of complaints about it.

"Instead of taking care of it, they gave us mesh gloves, because a lot of us were getting cut in the hands. But when you put a mesh glove on a knife hand, you might as well grease the knife. Live hogs were kicking our knives out of our hands. Next, they gave us finger rings that were attached to the knife. When a hog kicks you, the knife stays in your hand. So instead of a flying knife, you've got a double-edged blade flopping around in your hand."

Van Winkle turned his head to the right and lifted his chin to show me a scar on his neck.

"I got cut across my jugular," he said. "I was scared, scared to death. Stitches go with the territory in a packing house. I can live with stitches. I can live with getting cut once in a while. What I can't live with is cutting my own throat.

"After I cut my neck I told the foreman, 'I'm not here to die, I'm not going to stick any more hogs for you.' I met with management and told them, 'You can't force me to stick live hogs. The law states I don't have to do something I feel puts my life in jeopardy. Well, my life's in jeopardy so I'm not sticking any more hogs.'

"I felt a little bad because I knew someone would have to do the job, someone else's life would be in danger. I figured, if the foreman wants live hogs stuck, let him do it. So you know who the main foreman replaced me with?" Van Winkle closed his eyes and shook his head. "His own son.

"As a member of the union negotiating team I had access

to corporate executives. This problem is no secret to them," he said. "They didn't do anything so I went to the USDA—some sympathetic inspectors low on the totem pole. We found out that was a joke. They'd say, 'There's nothing we can do about it. Nothing we can do.' Then they'd walk off.

"So I go to their supervisor, a USDA veterinarian, and tell him workers are being hurt by live hogs. I try to make him see how much cruelty to the animals was going on. He'd be like, 'Hey, I'm coming down.' And he'd tell everyone in advance. The main foreman would tell me the vet was coming down, then he'd crank up the stunners, walk around picking up pipes and warning everybody, 'Whatever you do, don't use no pipes, the government man is coming down.' The vet would look around and say, 'I don't see no live hogs.' After that, he'd tell anyone who complained, 'Hey, I've been down there, I've seen it. There's nothing wrong with them hogs.'

"I go to Iowa's Occupational Safety and Health Administration. They said they have no statutes covering live hogs, which means no way of governing that. When OSHA would arrange to inspect the plant, here comes management again, turning up the stunners, taking away the pipes, making everything look nice. The foremen even made sure everybody had their earplugs in."

"Wouldn't it be easier for management and everyone else just to fix the problem?" I asked.

Van Winkle shrugged. "Might cost them a dime. Why protect workers when you can replace them? So we've got a few hundred complaints about the problem over the last few years. So we've got a guy sitting in the hospital with a hundred twenty-five stitches in his face—so what? There are a hundred people out there waiting for that sticker's job. Morrell's getting the pigs they want, they're making the money they want.

"I left Morrell's because I couldn't stand seeing what they were doing to people anymore. As safety representative I'd get small concessions from management once in a while," he said, "but when it came to the important problems, like people being mutilated and animals treated cruelly, they'd refuse to do anything. I couldn't stand by and watch any longer. I had to get out."

The waitress refilled our coffee cups and asked if we wanted anything else. We both said no. I hadn't touched my muffin.

"I was supposed to interview another guy last night," I told Van Winkle, "but he was in jail. Arrested for assault."

"That's not uncommon," he said. "The worst thing, worse than the physical danger, is the emotional toll. If you work in that stick pit for any period of time, you develop an attitude that lets you kill things but doesn't let you care. You may look a hog in the eye that's walking around down in the blood pit with you and think, God, that really isn't a bad-looking animal. You may want to pet it. Pigs down on the kill floor have come up and nuzzled me like a puppy. Two minutes later I had to kill them—beat them to death with a pipe. I can't care.

"When I worked upstairs taking hogs' guts out, I could cop an attitude that I was working on a production line, helping to feed people. But down in the stick pit I wasn't feeding people. I was killing things. My attitude was, it's only an animal. Kill it.

"Sometimes I looked at people that way, too," he said. "I've had ideas of hanging my foreman upside down on the line and sticking him. I remember going into the office and telling the personnel man that I have no problem pulling the trigger on a person—if you get in my face I'll blow you away.

"Every sticker I know carries a gun, and every one of them would shoot you. Most stickers I know have been arrested for assault. A lot of them have problems with alcohol. They *have* to drink, they have no other way of dealing with killing live, kicking animals all day long. If you stop and think about it, you're killing several thousand beings a day."

"How did you deal with it?" I asked.

"By the time I was sticking at Morrell I was already in Alcoholics Anonymous. That gave me outlets, I could go to people and talk to them. But most men are taught not to do that. We don't share what's going on inside us. So a lot of guys at Morrell just drink and drug their problems away. Some of them end up abusing their spouses because they can't get rid of the feelings. They leave work with this attitude and they go down to the bar to forget. Only problem is, even if you try to drink those feelings away, they're still there when you sober up.

"When I told management I was leaving, they offered me a foreman's job," Van Winkle said. "I just laughed at them. They found out I was studying to be an RN, so they—"

"You're studying to be a *nurse*?"

He nodded. "Back in college. So Morrell offered me a nursing job. I told them I was going into nursing because I want to help people, not help destroy people. I said I wouldn't work in that capacity at Morrell's for all the money in the world.

"Once in a while, when school gets too rough, I go take a tour at Morrell's. Same pigs, same people, same jobs: none of them's changed. I do this because I realize that if I don't study, I'll end up back there.

"Last time I went down there I saw the same live hogs— nothing's changed. There are a few different faces, but all the expressions are the same."

※   ※   ※

Ed Van Winkle no longer worked at Morrell, and Vladak and Jansson could only speak for the night shift. I wanted to find someone who could document conditions on the day shift.

On a bitterly cold night, eleven degrees with a blustery north wind, I drove the hilly streets of Sioux City, Iowa, looking for the address of Donny Tice, the day-shift sticker Tommy Vladak had told me about. Over the phone, Tice's voice had a deep, rich quality, like a late-night jazz-station deejay. When I knocked at his apartment, a tall, thin man in his mid-thirties with a receding hairline opened the door. He smiled and let me into his homey, nicely furnished living room, put on some soft music, and offered me a beer. I said no thanks and unpacked my tape recorder.

Tice sat down, opened a beer, lit a cigarette. The friendly smile was still on his face.

"You're doing a human-interest, life-in-the-slaughterhouse kind of thing?" he asked.

"Not exactly. I'm checking on violations of humane slaughter regulations," I explained.

"Jeez. I hope coming over here doesn't turn out to be a let-down for you."

"How do you mean?"

"I'm not a union member," he said.

"That's all right."

"No, I mean I don't know how much I can say." His smile was now apologetic. "I'd really like to help but I could lose my job for talking to you."

Damn. I turned off the tape recorder. "It's been a long day. Maybe I will have that beer."

The knot that was still lodged in my chest made swallowing painful. When I'd gone to the doctor he'd ordered me not to drink. But sharing a beer might loosen Tice up. He brought me a bottle from the kitchen.

"Do you have kids?" I asked.

"Two of them." He pulled out his wallet and showed me pictures of them. "Proud daddy."

We sat for a while trading banter. While the other men I'd talked to had regional accents and rural manners, Tice spoke unaccented urbanese in a confiding, almost sophisticated tone.

I noticed a purplish bruise among the tattoos on his arm.

"How'd you get that?"

"A hog I was sticking kicked me."

With his go-ahead, I turned the tape recorder back on. "Don't they get stunned before they come to you?"

"Some are completely missed by the stunners," he said. "Sometimes they get doubled up in the restrainer and the stunner misses the bottom hog. Sometimes the stun operator dozes off—I've actually seen him fall asleep on the job. He'll be stunning, his eyes start to droop, and then he nods off. I've thrown blood on him to wake him up." Tice laughed. "If he gets mad, I'll say, 'Sorry. Let me wash that off'—and turn the high pressure hose on him.

"Sometimes the stunner likes to play games with the shackler. He purposely doesn't stun hogs right so they'll be hard to shackle. He'll give the shackler a hog that's just a little testy so when he tries to hang it it'll kick and fall down into the pit."

"Isn't that dangerous for you?" I asked. "What do you do?"

"If I get a hog that's trying to eat my cookies," he replied, "I only have one chance to stick him. I'm not about to put my life in danger. I go in one time, hard.

"Sometimes I grab it by the ear and stick it right through the eye. I'm not just taking its eye out, I'll go all the way to the hilt, right up through the brain, and wiggle the knife. Instant rag doll.

"Hang on a second—" Tice said. He pulled a sticking dagger from a shelf and showed me how to stick a hog. For a few moments the room blurred out of focus. I found myself very alone, watching this man standing in front of me in his black leather boots, black jeans, and Harley-Davidson tank top, whipping a six-inch blade back and forth through the air a foot and a half from my face.

Finally he sat down again.

"Not to toot my own horn, but I'm real good at what I do. And you're right, it's a combat zone. Sometimes I get a premonition, a feeling like, 'You better be really good today, Donny, you better be on your toes, because this is the day you're going to get cut bad.' And I'm experienced enough to realize that if I do get cut, it's going to be serious. I've beaten the odds too many times.

"About a year ago," he continued, "I got knifed in the forehead. I was pulling my knife out of one hog and the hog next to it caught my hand, kicked so hard that when the knife hit my forehead, my head was thrown back. Luckily it was the flat of the blade. Scared me shitless."

We got to talking about the effect the job was having on him.

"I've taken out my job pressure and frustration on the animals, on my wife—who I almost lost—and on myself, with heavy drinking."

He downed another gulp of beer while I glanced around for signs of his wife.

"I actually thought I was going crazy at one point," he said. "I'd hit the bar after work every day, pound down four or five beers, come home and just sit and stare off into space through three or four more. If I talked at all, it was to bitch and chew. I was an SOB, royally. I mean gold-plated. My wife thought all this was directed at her. I'd want to tell her the truth, find the right words so she'd really understand, but I never could.

"Little things would set me off. I was putting a new alternator belt on my wife's car and the wrench slipped and I gouged my knuckle. I stood back and had a fit beating that car. I was beating it, kicking it, screaming at it. It was like I'd lost my mind."

"Where is your wife?"

"Driving to Lovelady, Texas," he replied. "I don't like her traveling alone, but she's got a loaded handgun next to her on the front seat. Checking out some jobs for us. I'm getting out of the pack. Eleven years is enough."

Tice went for another beer. I was still on my first.

"Down in the blood pit they say that the smell of blood makes you aggressive," he said as he walked back into the room. "And it does. You get an attitude that if that hog kicks at me, I'm going to get even. You're already going to kill the hog, but that's not enough. It has to suffer. When you get a live one you think, Oh good, I'm going to beat this sucker."

Tice was on autopilot now. I just let him talk.

"Another thing that happens is that you don't care about people's pain anymore. I used to be very sensitive about people's problems—willing to listen. After a while, you become desensitized. And as far as animals go, they're a lower life-form. They're maybe one step above a maggot.

"Like, one day the live hogs were driving me nuts and the kill-floor superintendent was playing his power games, yelling at me about something. I threw my knife on the floor, I'm screaming at him, 'Come on, you little pimple. You want a piece of me? Come on! Right now!' If he'd come down there I would've slit his throat. Could've taken a human life and not given it one thought or had one regret for it."

Tice had his beer bottle clasped in both hands in his lap and was staring straight ahead. His skin had gone pale. A smooth, perfectly vertical column of smoke rose like incense from the cigarette in the ashtray.

"It's the same thing with an animal who pisses you off, except it *is* in the stick pit, you *are* going to kill it. Only you don't just kill it, you go in hard, push hard, blow the windpipe, make it drown in its own blood. Split its nose. A live hog would be running around the pit. It would just be looking up at me and I'd be sticking, and I would just take my knife and —eerk—cut its eye out while it was just sitting there. And this hog would just scream.

"One time I took my knife—it's sharp enough—and I sliced off the end of a hog's nose, just like a piece of bologna. The hog went crazy for a few seconds. Then it just sat there looking kind of stupid. So I took a handful of salt brine and ground it into his nose. Now that hog really went nuts, pushing its nose all over the place. I still had a bunch of salt left on my hand—I was wearing a rubber glove—and I stuck the salt right up the hog's ass. The poor hog didn't know whether to shit or go blind.

"It's not anything anyone should be proud of," Tice said. "It happened. It was my way of taking out frustration.

"Another time, there was a live hog in the pit. It hadn't done anything wrong, wasn't even running around the pit. It was just alive. I took a three-foot chunk of pipe—two-inch diameter pipe—and I literally beat that hog to death. Couldn't have been a two-inch piece of solid bone left in its head. Basically, if you want to put it in layman's terms, I crushed his skull. It was like I started hitting the hog and I couldn't stop. And when I finally did stop, I'd expended all this energy and frustration, and I'm thinking, what in God's sweet name did I do?"

Tice looked at me again, and seemed to snap out of his confessional trance.

"But I wasn't the only guy doing this kind of stuff," he said. "One guy I work with actually chases hogs into the scalding tank. And everybody—hog drivers, shacklers, utility men—uses lead pipes on hogs. Everybody knows it, all of it."

"Including management?" I asked.

"Right. They make sure everything's by the book when anybody official visits. Whenever OSHA comes to check on things, the stick pit runs like a jewel. As soon they're gone it's back to business as usual.

"They even hide this stuff from their own consultants," he said. "The last time a consultant came in, the foreman said, 'Donny, do me a favor. Please don't stick any of them in the eye today. I don't want to lose my job.'

"People go into Morrell expecting respect and good working conditions. They come out with carpal tunnel, tendinitis, alcoholism, you name it, because they're put under incredible pressure and they're expected to perform under intolerable conditions. Or they develop a sadistic sense of reality. It used to be fun. Now it's a shit job."

"Fun?"

"Yeah," he replied. "You develop a bizarre sense of humor

down there. Like one guy. His elevator doesn't run all the way to the top floor, if you know what I mean. Last week, for a five-dollar bet, he drank a cup of blood. Think of all the diseases you could get."

"That's disgusting," I said.

"I've got a reputation for sucking on eyeballs," he admitted.

"You're dumping on a guy for drinking blood, and you're sucking on eyeballs?"

We both started laughing, then stopped short.

"How come you're willing to tell me these things?" I asked.

"Like they say," Tice replied, "if you're not part of the solution, you're part of the problem."

I turned off the tape recorder and got ready to leave. I didn't hate Donny Tice. But I hated what he was doing. I probably should have been afraid to be alone with him. For his part he seemed relieved to have gotten his sins off his chest.

I said good night and left.

8

Blood-Red and Frozen

The next night, I picked up Donny Tice and drove to an apartment complex on the outskirts of town. Alec Wainwright would speak more freely, Tice had told me, if he was there, too.

Wainwright and his girlfriend were in his second-floor apartment watching football on TV. The girlfriend changed channels when Wainwright, Tice, and I moved to the kitchen to talk.

Not yet out of his teens, Wainwright had already been working as a day-shift shackler for two years.

Wainwright talked about the same games as Tice had—the stun operator would intentionally misstun hogs so that Wainwright would have a hard time shackling them.

"Sometimes," he said, "when the chain stops for a little while and we have time to screw around with the hog, we'll half stun it. It'll start freaking out, going crazy. It'll be sitting there yelping."

Other times, when a hog would get loose outside the catch pen, he said, he and his co-workers would chase it up to the scalding tank and force it to jump in. "When that happens," he said, "we tell the foreman the hog accidentally jumped in."

Wainwright had little new to add to what Tice had already told me, but he did confirm Tice's claims of gratuitous cruelty to the animals. And while Tice's confession had seemed both painful and cathartic for him, Wainwright, in telling me of his atrocities against the already doomed pigs, chortled with delight as if recounting a schoolboy prank.

"Why do you do it?" I asked.

"Because it's something to do," Wainwright said. "Like when our utility guy takes the ol' bar and beats the hell out of the hogs in the catch pen. That's kind of fun. I do it, too."

"How often do you do that?"

"I dunno," he replied. "It just depends if Donny's in the mood or not. Sometimes he wants them knocked, and some-times he don't care. Like today, you were—"

"Didn't care," Tice said. "I was in a good mood."

"Okay," I said. "So hogs may be shackled conscious, or piped and shackled, or they might even be stuck on the floor of the stick pit?"

"Done that before," Tice said. "Blood's gushing out. They'll run around and then pretty soon they'll sit down, then they'll act like Stevie Wonder," he said, waving his head from side to side. "And the next thing you know, flop. Over they go."

"That's the funnest thing," said Wainwright. "I like watch-ing that. Eric got a kick out of that the other day when he watched that."

After we left Wainwright's, Tice asked me out for a beer. I dropped him off at his house and went back to my motel instead.

* * *

Mike Huntsinger introduced me to Clay Calkin, an unlikely-looking hog sticker. A quiet, courteous man whose wife worked for the local school system, Calkin confirmed what the others had told me. He also offered to take me to "Red" Martin, a Morrell veteran I kept hearing about and wanted to meet.

The screen door slammed behind me. In the dark living room a woman and several children sat watching TV. Calkin led me to the kitchen where a muscular man with tattooed arms and a fiery look in his eyes was sitting at the table. In his ten years at John Morrell, Red Martin had worked many jobs on the kill floor, including two years as a sticker.

"I paid for every minute of it, too," he said in a gravelly voice. "Alcoholism, arthritis. Got hung up in the hoist shackling live hogs, trying to keep the product moving. That's their big concern. When it comes to people, they don't give a shit."

He glared at me, as if daring me to take issue with his opinions or his way of expressing them.

"Everybody warned me about you, Red," I said.

He cracked a small smile.

"I'm not at the top of the popularity list at Morrell. I been fired five times, and I'm not afraid to talk. I'll sit right there and call 'em damn liars to their faces."

Martin echoed the others' complaints about live hogs on the chain, but was more interested in talking about crippled animals.

"If a hog can't walk, they scoop the son of a bitch up on a

dead run with a Bobcat [small tractor]. Whupp!" he exclaimed. "Right up in the air. If he stays in the bucket, he stays in. If he falls out, you run him over, or pin him up against the wall, finish busting the rest of his legs so he can't run any further."

The two men got to talking about driving hogs up the chutes.

"Hogs are stubborn," Martin said. "Beating them in the head seems to work about the best. Piece of rebar [concrete reinforcement bar] about an inch across, you force a hog down the alley, have another guy standing there with a piece of rebar in his hand—"

"Yeah, it's like playing baseball," Calkin said.

Martin laughed. "Yep, just like somebody pitching something at you."

Martin got back onto the subject of cripples, and the state of animals when they arrived at Morrell.

"They leave cripples laying all over the place," he said. "They run hogs on top of them. And they don't keep deads picked up. Over the weekend, the deads'll turn fat, green, and ugly. You go out there, you got a hangover, and you know what sick is." Both men laughed.

"Another thing is, in the winter, some hogs come in all froze to the sides of the trucks. They tie a chain around them and jerk them off the walls of the truck, leave a chunk of hide and flesh behind. They might have a little bit of life left in them," he said, "but workers just throw them on the piles of dead ones. They'll die sooner or later, because there's nothing left to them."*

---

*Farm animals are routinely trucked long distances in harsh weather (extreme cold or heat).

Several people had mentioned that Morrell periodically hired an independent consultant to inspect its plant, a highly respected Ph.D. who also maintained close ties to the animal protection community. I knew this consultant. She had a national reputation as a slaughter expert.

"Were you at work the day the consultant came to inspect the plant?" I asked him. "She said she came in unannounced and found everything was fine, no violations."

"Unannounced? Bullshit. We had two days' notice. They came around, 'Clean this up, pick that up, don't leave those around.'"

＊　＊　＊

Toby Glenn, a meatpacking employee for ten years, was also a union official. I asked him about the transport of hogs.

"In the summer they crowd them in trucks and run them clear from Canada," he said. "They don't stop and spray them to cool them down, so you get a lot of them that die from the heat.

"In winter after a long run like that, they always got ten to fifteen dead, frozen hogs laying around. Sometimes there's a pile of hogs laying there when I go to work, and when I get off work at 5 P.M., that same pile of hogs is still lying there. All day. A lot of times there's live ones in there."

"With the frozen ones?" I asked.

"Oh, sure. You could see them still lifting their heads up, looking around. Their bodies would be blood-red from being froze so hard."*

---

*When hogs arrive frozen at slaughterhouses—which is a common occurrence—their protections under the Humane Slaughter Act are mysteriously waived. Since they are of no value for human con-

Because Glenn was also a member of the union's safety committee, he could go to areas of the plant that otherwise would have been off-limits. He was the first to talk about the rendering area, where condemned hogs are ground up and cooked down for use in animal feed, fertilizer, and other products. "It's not uncommon to find a live hog in rendering," he said. "Sometimes there are ten hogs piled up, and sometimes a live hog is buried under the pile of dead ones."

"Are you telling me that hog gets ground up alive?" I asked.

"Unless somebody takes it upon himself to beat it in the head with a pipe or a hammer to put it out of its misery," he replied.

*   *   *

George Blomquist had worked at the plant for over four years in a variety of jobs, including a two-week stint a few months earlier disposing of DOA (dead on arrival) hogs.

"You're going to lose hogs in a semi[trailer] no matter what, from getting suffocated or from being too hot or too cold," he said. "During the time I worked in rendering, there was large piles of dead hogs every day. They must've been losing fifteen to twenty out of each truckload."

"What do you do with them?"

"Well, when they come off the truck, they're solid as a block of ice. Sometimes they'd be so froze that you'd have to

---

sumption, antemortem inspectors neither examine them nor make a decision as to their disposition. Nor are they provided shelter or promptly stunned. Instead they are left to fend for themselves until they die.

take a hot water hose to thaw them apart before you were able to chain-saw them. Then you take an ax-chopper or a chain saw and split the backbone in three places so it won't wreck the auger*."

"You ever see any live hogs with the frozen ones?" I asked.

Blomquist didn't look comfortable with this question, and thought about it a while before answering. "Well, they're supposed to be dead when they come back there. I thought, anyway. I went to pick up some hogs one day for chainsawing from a pile of about thirty frozen hogs, and I found two frozen alive hogs in that pile. What I'm saying is they were frozen, but they were still alive. It was about minus 77° windchill outside, and I believe they'd just traveled down from Canada. We'd been unloading bones [to be ground up for bone meal] for several hours, so I guess they'd been lying in that pile for about three hours."

"And the way that you could tell they were alive is they—"

"Oh," he interrupted. "I could tell they were alive because they raised their heads up like, 'Help me.' Like they were saying, 'Somebody's going to have to do something to help me.' "

"But they were frozen?"

"Like a block of ice. Breathing real slow. It wasn't much longer before they died. They were off to the side of the pile; somehow they had managed to move themselves there. They were raising their heads looking at me. And wishing I'd put them out of their misery. So that's what I did. I had no authority to do that, but I took it upon myself because I couldn't stand it.

---

*A giant corkscrew that slowly forces meat or by-products through a grinder.

"If I was laying in a pile and freezing to death and I couldn't move, I'd rather have you kill me than just leave me there. I don't think hogs should have to suffer like that."

"How'd you do it?" I asked.

"I took my ax-chopper and chopped them to death. Hit them in the head. One bang and that was it," he said. "The whole thing made me sick.

"I told my supervisor that they'd been frozen alive and that I'd killed them. He said, 'Oh, that's fine.' All I could think of was, what is wrong with these people? You got to walk past dead hogs every day on your way to the employee parking lot."

＊   ＊   ＊

I couldn't imagine anyone working year after year in a job that required them to torture animals and subject themselves to constant physical danger. I understood that people needed jobs; I didn't understand why they put up with these conditions. Wasn't that what unions were for?

The next day I asked union official Mike Huntsinger about it.

"We've brought up the problem of conscious hogs to management's attention thirty-five or forty times in the last five years," he said, and gave me a list of all the managers to whom complaints were made.

With no response from management, Huntsinger had contacted the Iowa Department of Labor about the hazards of working in the blood pit. An inspector visited the plant but took no action.

"These are human beings and they need help!" the local union president wrote the state. "It's inhumane to subject man or beast to these conditions. We are reaching out for help!"

I asked Mike why the union hadn't brought the humane violations to the USDA's attention. Neither he nor the other local union officials were aware that the USDA had any enforcement authority regarding the humane treatment of livestock, or that there even was a Humane Slaughter Act.

Not knowing where else to turn, Huntsinger had contacted the local animal shelter. They'd forwarded Huntsinger's complaint to the Iowa Department of Agriculture, which sent it on to the USDA. According to the response I received to a Freedom of Information Act request, the USDA veterinarian in charge at Morrell, Dr. Daniel T. Leonard, replied with a one-paragraph Speed-memo to his supervisor: "I've observed slaughter procedures and have seen no problems with sticking hogs at this speed. I will continue to monitor sticking procedures. If problems occur, immediate action will be taken. I do not feel we have a problem at this time."

PART THREE

THE "SLAUGHTERHOUSE EIGHT"

9

Beyond the Law

There are a lot of unwanted horses in this country. In fact, according to the USDA, each year in the United States, between one and three hundred thousand pleasure and race horses find themselves at the business end of the captive bolt gun. While a small percentage of horsemeat may end up in pet food, today most is shipped to Europe where it is sold in meat cases for about $6.00 a pound. And every one of those horses is inspected at U.S. taxpayer expense.

Most horses slaughtered in the United States are young, healthy animals whose owners simply have no use for them. During a visit to a horse auction, however, one can also usually see many broken-down, mistreated, and emaciated animals, horses whose owners have neglected them. Nothing more than a financial burden to their owners, such animals are

simply hauled off to auction barns where "killers"—slaughterhouse buyers—pay around fifty-five cents a pound. Thus,
instead of being penalized for the cruelty they've inflicted,
irresponsible horse owners are rewarded with a slaughterhouse check.

For over a year I'd spent weekends documenting the conditions of slaughter-bound horses at auction houses. With
photos showing the animals' conditions—broken bones,
burns, infections, starvation so severe they could barely stand
up—we'd finally convinced a prosecutor to raid a horse auction and prosecute the abusers. And that's why I'd left Sioux
City, to head back East to conduct the raid.

Someone in the sheriff's office had tipped off the auction
house the day before the raid. We went ahead with the bust anyway, arrested an alleged abuser, seized some horses, and got
national news coverage that brought the issue to public attention.

The real victory was that the raid happened at all. While
every state in the Union has an anticruelty statute on the
books making it a crime to treat an animal in an "unneces-
sarily cruel fashion" or to deprive it of sustenance or intentionally torture it, I'd learned early on in my career that
trying to convince prosecutors to file cruelty charges against
animal abusers can be very difficult.

To begin with, many inhumane practices—even when bla-
tantly contrary to the intent of anticruelty statutes—are
exempt from anticruelty laws. Whether it's the quarter of a billion male chicks—of no commercial value in egg production—that the poultry industry intentionally grinds up alive or
smothers each year, or the millions of breeding hogs and veal
calves that spend their entire lives inside crates so small they
can never turn around, these and billions of other farm animals

are generally exempted from the law's coverage under the wastebasket term "normal agricultura_ practices."

*   *   *

The question now was: should we try to convince local prosecutors to file animal-cruelty charges against Kaplan and Morrell or should we expand the investigation's scope in the hope of exposing violations and improving conditions in slaughterhouses across the United States?

And what would we have to do to win convictions in agricultural towns like Bartow, Florida, or Sioux City, Iowa? First, convincing a prosecutor to take the case would be even more difficult than usual, since USDA inspectors were already on the slaughterhouse premises supposedly enforcing the Humane Slaughter Act.

Even if a prosecutor accepted the case, he or she might plea-bargain it down to nothing. Or a case could be dismissed on a technicality, or the defendants acquitted by a jury of sympathizers. I'd certainly seen that happen before.

To make things even tougher, the physical evidence had already been butchered, packaged, and sent to meat cases across the country. If law officers entered Kaplan's or Morrell's premises with a search warrant, any evidence of the alleged violations could miraculously disappear. And we could be almost certain that USDA personnel would testify on management's behalf. To do otherwise would be to incriminate themselves.

Even if we were able to gain a conviction, just how far would it go? Another Morrell plant—this one located in Sioux Falls, South Dakota—had already been slapped with one of the nation's largest penalties for worker safety violations, and corporate officials there had allowed the safety hazards to persist. The $1,500 maximum fine for animal abuse in Iowa wouldn't even make a dent in the company's petty cash.

Besides, while interviewing Morrell employees, I'd been given information about more possible violations at that other Morrell slaughterhouse ninety miles up the road in South Dakota. From another source, I received a lead about a Midwest horse plant where horses were allegedly being beaten and stuck alive. And I received a complaint from a Virginia pig hauler who, among the many abuses he listed, was most disturbed by the bodiless pigs' legs he'd seen littering the unloading dock. "Yesterday, I saw two more legs that had been cut off," he wrote. "They were left in a mud walkway between the trucks. That's the third time I've seen the legs lying there like that. I've asked other drivers, but they know nothing about it."

And every time I called Timothy Walker from the road to describe the case that seemed to be developing against the USDA, he would respond with something like, "I told you, Gail. When I complained to my supervisors about Kaplan's, they said to me, 'Those problems exist all over the country.' "

It seemed to me that the only way to effect permanent change at slaughterhouses would be to expose to the public the USDA's role in allowing violations to persist. Thus, my first order of business was to document violations at more plants. Then, and as soon as possible, we would release our findings through the national media in a way that would both expose the USDA and make Congress demand compliance across the board.

*   *   *

Still, I just couldn't walk away from Sioux City without doing something for the animals who would soon be on their way there. If I went directly to Morrell management or the press my investigation would be revealed and my informants put at risk, probably to no avail. Instead I called Morrell's independent consultant—the slaughter expert and colleague of mine who'd inspected the plant. I wanted to make sure she knew what was *really* going on. After speaking with a few of my sources, she agreed to bring the charges up to Morrell executives without disclosing where she'd gotten the information. I'd hoped that once advised by their own consultant, plant officials would take action if, for no other reason, than to prevent information about the atrocities from leaking out.

And they did—sort of. I got a call from Clay Calkin, one of the Morrell stickers I'd interviewed. "Management made us sign statements of humaneness," he reported. "But that was just to cover their butts. I mean, *they're* the ones that keep turning the stunner current down.

"Just today," he continued, "a hog trying to get away jumped into the scalding tank. A bunch of other hogs were jammed in the restrainer so tight they couldn't move. The drivers were prodding the shit out of them. Finally, they dropped the hoist down—didn't stun them or nothing—got a shackle around one of the hogs' legs and tried to pull him out. Ripped the meat right off the hog's leg, down to the bone. These guys had signed that statement," he said. "And two Morrell supervisors stood there directing the whole thing."

※   ※   ※

Until recently, I'd always been very physically fit. But now I had such a lump in my throat that I could barely swallow. My shoulders were so tense, they were up to my ears; I was having difficulty breathing, and the lump in my throat was keeping me up nights. Still, I worked frantically transcribing tape after tape, writing up affidavits. That is, except those lunch hours that were spent at the doctor's office drinking chalky cocktails in front of a fluoroscope.

"This adult white female has a recent history of episodic feelings of shortness of breath," my doctor wrote in his report, "a feeling of air hunger that she has difficulty describing. Over the course of the last year, she has had a problem where she felt there was a knot in her chest and had a feeling of a lump in her throat. The patient is under a tremendous amount of stress at work, both due to the fact that she has to work long hours on a particularly difficult project and also because the nature of the work is very upsetting."

After watching the chalky cocktail work its way through my insides, the doctor said he wanted a closer look and scheduled me for further tests. At the hospital they stuck a tiny video camera down my throat and looked around.

The endoscopy turned up nothing. My doctor diagnosed stress.

*   *   *

My degree is in what's called Natural Resource Conservation, but the curriculum focused more on efficient exploitation of the natural world than preserving it. My first job out of college, with a state fish and game agency, consisted of guiding hunters and fishermen to their prey. Next, while freelancing as a nature writer and illustrator, I spent years sending my résumé to animal-protection professionals. Only after an article I'd written for the *New York Times* helped push through an animal-protection measure that the humane community had been trying to get passed for years, was I finally offered a job by the nation's largest animal protection organization, located in Washington, D.C. I snapped it up.

My first position was writer/editor, and I was responsible for compiling articles, newsletters, and membership materials describing horrific abuses committed against animals. But one can only write about systematic exploitation for so long. As many familiar with human or animal abuse issues know, the more you learn about what's really going on out there in the world, the more compelled you are to get out there and do something about it. After several years as a writer, I was finally promoted to investigator. This work I was doing—exposing offenses against animals—was exactly what I wanted to do in life.

❋   ❋   ❋

Although I planned to do more investigating, I thought the time was right to touch base with a producer at CBS's "60 Minutes." I felt it would be helpful to get a commitment from a network to produce the story before I headed off to another slaughterhouse.

"This is the first time packing plant employees have ever gone public with information about what's really taking place on the kill floors of America's federally inspected slaughterhouses," I wrote. "And, if the USDA has its way, it will also be the last," I said, explaining that Timothy Walker had already been fired from USDA after speaking out about violations at the Kaplan packing plant.

Although swamped with other projects, the producer expressed mild interest in the story. I promised to keep him posted on developments as they occurred. And then I headed back to the field to check out my leads.

10

Slunks, Haulers, and "Too-Dead" Cows

Dear Ms. Eisnitz:

This is in reference to your Freedom of Information Act request. . . . The John Morrell Company in Sioux Falls, South Dakota, has no records of any violations of the Federal Humane Slaughter Act.

—Sincerely,
USDA

So far I had investigated violations at Morrell's pig slaughterhouse in Sioux City, Iowa. But the other John Morrell plant I had been told about—this one in Sioux Falls, South Dakota, ninety miles up the road—was the nation's only remaining large tri-species plant, slaughtering several thousand cattle, hogs, and sheep each day on three separate kill floors.

117

Despite the fact that it was one of the biggest slaughter-houses in the country, the USDA had not one report of a steer being improperly stunned; not one reference to pigs being excessively prodded or sheep being struck with pipes; no notations about disabled animals being dragged with cables. And in frigid South Dakota, where windchills often reach eighty degress below zero, there wasn't a mention of a single animal arriving frozen alive.

This was the plant that, in the late 1980s, had incurred near record OSHA fines after the company dramatically increased its line speeds. First, in 1986, OSHA investigated the plant for record-keeping violations and later slapped it with a fine of $690,000—OSHA's third highest penalty at the time. Then, in 1987, the plant's injury and illness rate soared to nearly 90 percent—meaning there were nearly 90 injuries and illnesses for every 100 workers at the plant. The following year, the *New York Times* reported that "John Morrell remains a case study in stubbornness of industrial safety problems." Still, instead of taking significant action to improve hazardous conditions, management continued to operate production lines at meteoric rates. OSHA slapped the plant with a second citation, this one for $4.3 million for willful violations of worker safety codes.*

Would a plant that had allowed its employees to become injured and maimed really care about the suffering of animals

---

*John Morrell & Company contested both citations. In a formal 1990 settlement with the company, OSHA reduced the severity of and dropped the fine in the first citation but required Morrell to pay $990,000 for the second citation. Sources: *New York Times,* Sunday, August 21, 1988, sec. 3, pp. 1, 8; OSHA Scan Report, U.S. Department of Labor, June 26, 1997.

or compliance with the law? Could a plant that was notorious for chewing up employees and then spitting them out really not have had a single humane violation in the past five years?

🐾   🐾   🐾

Sioux Falls, in the southeast corner of sparsely populated South Dakota, was fast becoming an island of fast-food joints, strip malls, and casinos in a vast sea of farmland. Once I'd been there a few days, though, I could sense the city's frontier-town beginnings, its rich Native American heritage, its rural roots, and its strong sense of community pride.

From outside the state penitentiary atop a hill on the edge of town, I got a clear view—and a strong whiff—of the sprawling old slaughterhouse that was Morrell. With steam billowing from stacks day and night and wooden tunnels climbing several stories high, the seventy-five-year-old brick-and-concrete complex looked more like a ramshackle factory than a packing plant.

Just across the street from the packing plant was the Sioux Falls Stockyard. Livestock were driven from the yard through what was called the Tunnel of Death, an underground passageway that led directly to the plant. Once in the plant, the animals were prodded up cleated ramps to the top floor. Then they were slaughtered and conveniently butchered, processed, and packaged by workers as they made their way down to the ground floor.

My first stop in town was the Labor Temple, the city's union hall, housing the offices of the United Food and Commercial Workers Union local, which represented Morrell workers.

I sat on the sofa in the Temple's lounge, an obvious outsider. The day-shift employees had just knocked off and were
coming in to drink coffee, smoke cigarettes, and talk. I introduced myself to a man who sat down next to me and told him
outright what I was doing there. I expected wariness or suspicion, but he invited me into the union's private conference
room, rounding up several more workers on the way.

The five men and three women—the Slaughterhouse
Eight, as I came to think of them—were different from the
employees I'd met at Morrell's Iowa plant. These were old-
timers who'd worked at Morrell their entire adult lives. For
years they'd been telling each other what they'd seen and
done in the plant. Now, for the first time, they were telling an
outsider.

We all settled in around the table with our cups of coffee.
Some of them lit cigarettes. Bucky White, a thin, handsome
man with an occasional wink, seemed to be the ringleader of
this group of friends. With his cowboy boots, slicked-back gray
hair, and a cigarette dangling from his lips, he looked like the
Marlboro Man. I asked him how long he'd worked at Morrell.

"Twenty-seven years," he said, "twenty-one of them
heading and sticking cattle."

"Is there ever a problem with knocking them?" I asked.
"Do they ever regain consciousness?"

White and a couple of the others laughed. Someone
grunted in disgust.

"I get a lot of live cattle out on the rail," White said.
"Sometimes they've knocked them and rolled them out [into
the shackling area] and they get up running and make it out
through the gate to the beef kill."

"First time I seen that," said Larry, a kill-floor worker with a round, lively face, "I go, 'What in the hell is going on?' The guy's running after a damn cow, and I hadn't seen the cow yet—it was already down by the viscera pan [where inspectors examine the animals' entrails]. All I see is a guy screaming and hollering."

Larry's mouth and eyes were wide open in mock stupefaction, and everybody else was laughing.

Margie White, Bucky's wife, said, "You should have seen it the day a hog got in there, running around on the beef kill. They were trying to lasso it."

"How often do these live animals get through the stunning process?" I asked.

"The way I look at it," White said, "out of the 1,228 beef I stuck today it would have been okay if a few were still alive. But it's all day. Constantly, all day, I get live cattle."

"This is going to sound like a silly question," I said, "but I have to ask it. How can you tell if the animal is conscious?"

"The live ones you could tell 'cause they're bellowing, blinking, looking around," he replied. "When you go to reknock them, they'll try to pull their head away from you. I move my hand, they move their head. I move this way, they move that way."

Larry was laughing. "That's why he gets paid so much. It's hard to hit a moving target."

Margie wasn't laughing. "He don't get paid enough."

"They'll hold their heads straight up and look at you," Rod Owen, another plant worker, said.

"A month ago Bucky got kicked in the mouth," Margie said.

White pointed to his lip. "Right here, just about drove my tooth right through. Then I got kicked behind the ear."

"Two weeks ago he got it right above the eye," Margie said.

"So in the last month," I asked, "how many times did you get nailed?"

"Got kicked in the mouth, the eye—"

"Under the arm," Margie said. "And just yesterday, underneath the other arm, it's black and blue. And what about your thumb? How long ago was that one?"

"Who have you complained to about this?" I asked.

Margie laughed derisively.

"The foreman," White said.

"And what has he done?"

"Nothing," White said. "Absolutely nothing."

"How many times have you complained?"

"Daily," he said. "Too many live cattle on the chain."

I asked White what the problem with the stunning was. He explained that the captive bolt knocking guns they used have two sizes of bolts. Plant management requires that the smaller, less effective bolt be used.

"We got a superintendent who claims the big bolt kills the cattle 'too dead' and they don't bleed properly." White shook his head. "I've headed [skinned the heads of] and stuck cattle for twenty-one years, and I've never heard of cattle being too dead."

"They're climbing up the walls and kicking you," Margie said. "But they're too dead."

I'd heard this "too dead" business in Sioux City, too, as another reason to turn down the stun current. It's an industry myth that an animal's heart has to keep beating in order to pump all the blood from its muscles. When blood is retained in the meat, it provides a good medium for bacteria to grow, and that reduces the meat's shelf life. I'd looked up several studies* in the National Agricultural Library and found that in the early eighties, researchers had proved beyond a shadow of a doubt that killing an animal by stopping the heart instead of just stunning it has no effect on the amount of blood retained in the meat. Yet the "too dead" idea lives on.

"Another thing," White went on, "every time you pull that trigger it takes four to six seconds for the pressure to build back up big enough to knock the next beef properly. The guy who does the knocking, he's constantly triggering the device."

"He'll knock the first one," Larry said, "and while he's moving to the next one, he's going kachunk, kachunk, just triggering it into the air. It's a habit with him."

"And the next beef he hits, it'll knock it down," White added, "but it don't do it as good as it's supposed to. The gun's old, and worn, and leaks. And they turn the air pressure down."

"Plus you have to knock them in the right spot," Margie said. "Not in the eye. Not in the ear."

White circled a small point in the center of his forehead with his fingers. "Right there, that's the whole area. Just that far off in any direction and that beef ain't stunned properly. Then you might have to knock it four or five times, and then

---

*B. B. Chrystall, C. E. Devine, and K. G. Newton, "Residual Blood in Lamb Muscles," *Meat Science* 5 (1980–1981): 339; A. H. Kirton, L. F. Frazerhurst, E. G. Woods, and B. B. Chrystall, "Effect of Electrical Stunning Method and Cardiac Arrest on Bleeding Efficiency, Residual Blood and Bloodsplash in Lambs," *Meat Science* 5 (1980–1981): 347; P. D. Warris, "The Residual Blood Content of Meat: A Review," *Journal of the Science of Food and Agriculture* 28 (1977): 457; P. D. Warris and S. B. Wotton, "Effect of Cardiac Arrest on Exsanguination in Pigs," *Research in Veterinary Science* 82 (1981).

you got problems. This knocker shoots them wherever he can in the head," he said. "He knows where to hit them, but it don't make no difference to him."

"He's a real airhead," Larry said. "You got to see him to believe him."

"Especially if he's in a hurry," White said, "if he's got to get caught up. Then I start getting a lot of live ones. That's how I got some live ones today; he couldn't get them knocked at all, so they open the gate this far and wrap a chain around its leg and hang it live."

"How do they drive cows onto the kill floor?" I asked.

"Electric prods," White said, "plugged into the wall."

Larry looked around the table. "Anybody ever been hit with one of them prods?"

A few nods, a "You betcha" from White.

"I caught one in the elbow one time," Larry said. "Holy shit does that hurt! I seen them take those stunners—they're about long as a yardstick—and shove it up the hog's ass."

"They do it with cows, too," Margie said.

"And in their ears—"

"Their eyes."

"Down their throat."

Larry shook his head. "They'll be squealing and they'll just shove it right down there. Even a hog don't deserve that."

"When they prod them too much," I said, "do they ever try to jump out of the knocking box?"

"Oh, sure," White said.

"And out of the drive alley,"* Margie said.

---

*The main passageway that extends from the pens toward the single-file chute that leads up to the stun area.

Larry tapped the side of his head. "They're not stupid animals. Just the guy that's knocking them's stupid."

They all laughed.

"And he's the best knocker you got, right?" Larry said.

White nodded. "According to the superintendent."

Larry tapped his head again. "The superintendent's [not too bright, either]. I've had to deal with all of these people. That's why I've earned my stripes." He stood up. "I've got to go."

After he left I asked about the hog kill. I was curious to find out whether the hogs here were being treated anything like those at Morrell's Iowa plant. Paul O'Day, one of the Slaughterhouse Eight who so far hadn't had much to say, had worked a short stint there as a driver after an injury.

"They beat cripples with pipes and stuff like that," he said. "Or stick a big hook up their butt and drag them. Or in their mouth. The roof of their mouth. And they're still alive. That's all I've seen."

Bucky White said, "I know they pull hogs out of trucks in the wintertime—"

"Frozen to the side of the trucks," O'Day said. "I don't know about the stunning and shackling, I was just driving them."

"See, a hog'll freeze in parts in a truck," White said. "They freeze to that steel railing. They're still alive, and they'll hook a cable on it and pull it out, maybe pull a leg off."

O'Day's wife, Chris—a tall, sturdy woman with long red hair—also worked on the beef kill. I asked her what job she performed.

"I just skin."

"Do you see—"

"I'm right there."

"She's twenty feet away from where I work," White said.

Then he shook his fist and mimicked a female voice. "Don't touch that beef, it's still alive! You shoot it first!"

"I'm telling him to put them out of their misery," she said. "It bothers me to hear them. You can hear them bellow. I mean, they're looking around, climbing the walls."

"How many?" I asked her.

"A lot."

Our meeting began to break up. The O'Days got up to leave, then sat back down when another worker, Chuck, came in. Two or three conversations were going at the same time. Rod Owen and Margie were talking about a window from which you could watch the knock box. From that window, Rod had counted six or seven conscious cattle shackled and hung in twenty minutes.

Bucky White and Chuck were counting off the people they'd complained to about conscious cows on the line.

"Every foreman in the joint," Chuck said. "Every mechanic who works on the guns."

Margie defected from her conversation to this one.

"Every supervisor."

"The assistant supervisor," White said. "Two mechanics, I don't know their last names—"

"Rob and Dale," Margie said.

"And one foreman supposedly told the superintendent over the beef division," White said.

"What about the USDA?" I asked.

Margie gave me a blank look. "Who?" The others cracked up.

"Do you ever see them?"

Most of them shook their heads.

"They're there," White said, "but they don't stop the line for live beef. Dr. Fanning's the only one who ever talked to me. He once asked me if I stick them in the heart or in the jugular vein."

"Why'd he ask that?" I said.

"I don't know."

"They ain't necessarily in there," Chuck said. "Inspectors are all on the other side of the building from where we're at."

"They can't see it," White said. "They don't want to be kicked or have a bull fall on them.*

"A lot of times," White said, changing the subject, "the leggers'll take their clippers and cut off the beef's leg right below the knee—the skinny part." He snuffed out his cigarette in an ashtray. "The beef'll continue to kick but it's not as much of a problem because it don't have that long of a reach."

"And they're still conscious?" I asked.

"Some of them."

※　※　※

Chris O'Day must have seen just as much as Bucky White had, yet she'd had little to say so far. Before we all left, I arranged to talk with her at her home that weekend.

The O'Days lived in a big farmhouse forty-five minutes out of town. As I pulled into the driveway I was greeted by a nanny goat, a couple of pet rabbits, and some children playing with the family dog—a scene straight out of Norman Rockwell.

O'Day led the way to her large kitchen where we sat down over coffee. With the rest of the bunch at that first meeting, she'd seemed so reserved—not shy or intimidated, just not

---

*Inspectors are much farther down the line inspecting heads at one station, organs at another, and carcasses at a third.

inclined to talk. I wondered if she'd disagreed with the Whites' version of what happens on the kill floor but didn't want to say so in front of them.

"How long have you worked at Morrell?" I asked her.

"Since '83, and on the beef kill since '89," she replied. "Before that I was in other departments."

"Have you seen beef hung alive or regain consciousness after—"

"Sure," she interrupted. "Their heads are up in the air, they're looking around, trying to hide. They've already been hit before by this thing, and they're not going to let it get at them again. They're swinging back and forth on one leg while Bucky's trying to hit them. As far as the ones that come back to life, it looks like they're trying to climb the walls. And that's *after* Bucky's stuck them.

"And then when they get to the leggers," she continued, "well, the leggers don't want to wait to start working on the cow until somebody gets down there to reknock it. So they just cut off the bottom part of the leg with the clippers. When they do that, the cattle go wild, just kicking in every direction."

※   ※   ※

It got to be a habit. For the next several days, every afternoon at around 3:15 I'd go down to the Labor Temple looking for my buddies. The Whites were often there—acting like best friends toward each other, like hard-boiled wiseacres toward everybody else—Rod Owen and his wife, and Pat Kelly, another union member who used to work at the plant and now was a garbage man. We'd go out for coffee or dinner, or just hang out at the temple.

I wanted to talk to the beef-kill knocker Ken Burdette, but because he was nonunion he never came to the Labor Temple. His phone number wasn't listed. Pat Kelly knew where he lived, though—Kelly was his garbage man. He drove me there one Saturday.

Ken Burdette was a big man who carried himself with confidence and had a smooth, easy charm He reminded me of the actor John Goodman. I introduced myself and Kelly, and explained what we were doing there.

Burdette introduced his wife, then looked at Kelly.

"I've seen you around."

"Out at the races."

"There you go."

Burdette told me he was willing to be interviewed on tape, sent his son for cigarettes, and invited us to sit down. I asked if he'd had problems stunning cattle.

"As the foremen speeded up the line, it got harder and harder to knock 'em. I have to hit 'em four or five times, see, and even then they sometimes still get up."

Like Bucky White, Burdette gave me a detailed explanation of the stun gun, telling me that the big bolt didn't do the job, so Morrell's "brilliant-minded people" switched to the smaller one. He also said they turned the air pressure down and didn't repair the gun when gaskets broke. "The air just pours out of there, sprays in your face. There's oil all in your face."

"When you say 'live cattle,'" I asked, "do you mean moving or kicking?"

"Like nerve reaction?" he asked. "No. They're conscious. Okay, when they turn their heads around when they're hanging upside down and they look at you, I guess that's one way you can tell they're alive. See, once they regain consciousness they start bellowing. They're hanging there going OOOAAAHH!"

"How many of them are like this?"

"Twenty-five to thirty percent, easy."

"Do they ever have to hang them alive?"

"Thousands of times," he said. "As long as you can get ahold of that leg, you bet. I could tell you horror stories."

"Please do."

"About cattle getting their heads stuck under the gate guards, and the only way you can get it out is to cut their heads off while they're alive."

"You've actually seen that?"

"I've *done* it," he said. "Just to keep the line moving. I've seen cows hit with whips, chains, shovels, hoes, boards. Anything they can use to move 'em. Seen them laid wide open across their nose and stuff.

"Cows that get hurt [in the transport or slaughter process], they call them 'haulers.' You take an electric winch, latch it on to one of her legs—it's supposed to be a leg—and drag her all the way through the kill alley to the knocking box. You can always tell them, because when they come out on the line, they're covered with—can I say it?"

"Sure." This big tough man was blushing.

"Cowshit," he laughed. "From being drug through the kill alley. If you couldn't get her leg, it would go around her neck, and by the time she gets up here she's almost dead—it's choking her. You're in such a hurry, and people get so mad at you if you don't get the job done on time, that your adrenaline's flowing and you don't care what you do to that animal."

Burdette's wife came back into the room. He looked at her for a few moments.

"I'd come home and be in a bad mood," he said. "Go right downstairs and go to sleep. Yell at the kids, stuff like that. One time I got really upset—she knows about this. A three-year-old heifer was walking up through the kill alley. And she was having a calf right there, it was half in and half out. I knew she was going to die, so I pulled the calf out. Wow, did my boss get mad."

"Slowed the line down?" I asked.

"No-no. They call these calves 'slunks,' " he explained. "They use the blood for cancer research [related to pharmaceuticals]. And he wanted that calf. What they usually do is when the cow's guts fall onto the gut table, the workers go along and rip the uterus open and pull these calves out. It's nothing to have a cow hanging up in front of you and see the calf inside kicking, trying to get out. This one, my boss wanted that calf, but I sent it back down to the stockyards."

"Did you ever complain about the way the animals are treated?" I asked. "Or about the conscious cows?"

"You bet. To the foremen, the inspectors, the kill floor superintendent. Even the superintendent over the beef division. We had a long talk one day in the cafeteria about this crap that was going on. I've gotten so mad some days I'd go and pound on the wall because they won't do anything about it."

"Do you ever see a USDA veterinarian down there?"

"No way. I've never seen a vet *near* the knocking pen. Nobody wants to come back there. See, I'm an ex-Marine. The blood and guts don't bother me. It's the inhumane treatment. There's just so much of it."

🐾   🐾   🐾

The Slaughterhouse Eight—mainly the Whites and the O'Days—introduced me to other workers who were willing to go on record with me.

"I've seen a lot of 'frozens,' " one stockyard worker said. "We get them in from Canada. I've seen as many as sixty dead ones off a truck."

Another worker told me that the employee in charge of cripples used a tractor at full speed to push disabled hogs down an alley. "One of them slid off to the side and hit a post. That hog was ripped wide open." Or, he smashes them into the cement wall to get them in the bucket. This same employee was often seen clubbing disabled hogs with pipes and beating them to death with boards. "He'd get mad at them," I was told. "He had a short fuse."

Another hog-kill worker told me that hogs would collapse from stress or exhaustion during the long journey through the plant. "These hogs are raised in confinement and the trip through the plant is probably a half-mile long. They've never walked like that in their lives." When they collapsed, drivers jabbed meat hooks in their mouths or anuses and dragged them through the chutes alive.

A worker mentioned that the foreman in the cattle yards beat cattle with pitchforks and brooms. "He'll kick them, fork them, use anything he can get his hands on. He's already broken three pitchforks so far this year, just jabbing them. He doesn't care if he hits its eyes, head, butt. He jabs them so hard he busts the wooden handles. And he clubs them over the back." Another employee explained that drivers near the beef kill were able to increase the current in their electric prods to three times the legal limit.

"I've seen live animals shackled, hoisted, stuck, and

skinned. Too many to count. Too many to remember," explained an official with the United Food and Commerical Workers Union local in Sioux Falls. "It's just a process that's continuously there. I've seen shackled beef looking around before they've been stuck. I've seen hogs [that are supposed to be lying down] on the bleeding conveyor get up after they've been stuck. I've seen hogs in the scalding tub trying to swim." The union official had spent years working in Morrell's beef, sheep, and pork divisions. "Animal abuse is so common that workers who've been in the industry for years get into a state of apathy about it. After a while it doesn't seem unusual anymore.

"In the wintertime there are always hogs stuck to the sides and floors of the trucks. They go in there with wires or knives and just cut or pry the hogs loose. The skin pulls right off. These hogs were alive when we did this. Animal abuse at Morrell is so commonplace nobody even thinks about it."

Despite his years of plant and union experience, the official didn't know until I told him that the USDA is responsible for enforcing the Humane Slaughter Act.

"Nobody knows who's responsible for correcting animal abuse at the plant. The USDA does zilch. Especially in the hog kill, where you have hogs going through at eleven hundred an hour, the abuse is totally out of control. The union's here to try to help the workers.* But nobody thinks about the suffering the *animals* go through."

---

*Organized labor suffered an unprecedented loss of power following Ronald Reagan's firing of 11,800 striking air traffic controllers in 1981. The administration's action, the resulting breakup of the Professional Air Traffic Controllers Organization union, and rulings by conservative judges at the time giving companies most of

Leaving Sioux Falls was different. Usually I left like a commando after a raid, getting out fast and quietly with my tapes and photos before anything hit the fan. This time I was leaving friends behind. We had a farewell dinner together, and I promised to stay in touch.

---

the advantages in strike situations, had a debilitating impact on U.S. labor unions. As a result, up until the successful Teamsters Union strike against UPS in 1997, labor unions, including those representing workers in packing plants, have struggled with limited success to effect change on behalf of their members.

11

A Trip to the State Pen

When I got back to Washington, I put together a compelling summary of the most graphic quotes from Kaplan and Morrell employees (present and former) and overnighted it to Mike Wallace's producer at "60 Minutes." I got a call from him the next day—he was very interested.

One of the statements that particularly impressed the producer had come out of a couple of phone interviews I'd done with a man who spent two years working as a sticker at a Midwest horse slaughter plant. The producer wanted me to visit the sticker in person and see if he'd agree to go on camera.

I arrived in Chicago during a driving rainstorm, rented a car, and headed west about two hours to the Dixon Correctional Center. At the prison I waited in a small room that smelled of Lysol. A guard came in, searched me from head to toe, then directed me to a chamber where a sliding steel door automatically closed behind me. A minute later another door slid open in front, and I walked into a well lit room where about a dozen inmates sat talking with family and friends.

The cinderblock room was large, had tables and chairs fixed in place, and there was a walled patio to my right. A guard sat in a booth high above the crowd where he could monitor every move.

I waited for what must have been an hour. Twice the buzzer sounded, signaling the half-hourly prisoner count. Each time the steel door rolled open and a young man was escorted in, I wondered if this was my informant. Steve Parrish finally entered and was directed to where I was seated.

Parrish, a compact, graceful African American man in his early thirties, crossed the room with a slow, confident gait. He sat down across from me, smiled, then asked—as if he were actually interested—how I was doing. I wanted to establish a good rapport, so we talked for a while about life in general, his specifically.

He had worked in slaughterhouses ever since he was a teenager. He didn't say much about his life on Chicago's streets, the dangerous crowd he ran with—or how he'd landed in jail *this* time.

I asked him what kind of horses were slaughtered at the plant where he'd worked.

"Belgians, Arabians, little ponies—all kinds. Long as it's a horse. Stolen horses, too."

"Stolen?" I asked. Lately at my job, I'd been getting a lot of complaints about horses that had been stolen from their owners and sold to slaughterhouses. Horse theft for slaughter seemed to be on the increase.

"Guys with their own trucks, they'd steal horses and bring them for us to kill and sell," he replied. "This one guy—I know him pretty well—he told me it's good money, stealing horses. Said I got lots of experience with horses, would I like to go with him sometime and steal some. I told him I'm not really into that."

"Where would he steal them from?" I asked.

"A lot of people own little farms they don't live on," he said, "just places where they hold horses and feed them. Pet horses, riding horses in good condition, some of them young. These guys would bring them in at night. We didn't have no night shift then. The boss needed more meat to ship to Belgium. We'd stay over after the USDA doc left, or go back in the middle of the night. The boss would have the accountant put an extra bonus on our checks, twenty dollars for each horse. We'd kill anything from thirty to forty horses at night."

"What about USDA inspections?"

"They weren't inspected."

"And the inspector wouldn't notice the extra horses in the morning?" I asked.

"Everything's moving so fast," he replied. "He'd never know."

"How many times did you do this?"

"Quite a few. Maybe ten times."

"How'd they handle horses that couldn't walk?" I asked.

"If he's down on the truck, down in the manure, and he don't want to move," he said, "or if the horse is injured or sick or pregnant, or maybe he's done a split and can't get up—you try to pull him up by the tail. Or stick a two-by-four under him, try to pick him up. Or hit him with the shocker. There are times we took a boning knife and stuck them in the rectum till they bleed to make them get up."

"Does this happen much?"

"A lot," he replied. "Because he's holding up progress. Plus you don't want the other horses to run all over him and trample him and bruise the meat up. So we'd take a hoist, put a chain around the horse's neck and drag him all the way to the holding pen. Or if we kick a horse and he is 2D—downed or disabled— and we can't move him, I'd split his throat in the pens and let him bleed, cut his nerves off at the back of his neck. Because you could work with him better when he's dead. You can bend his legs and you ain't got to worry about getting kicked. You can hold him and flip him and drag him to the knocking box. Either way, as long as we can get them to the kill floor."

"What about the ones who can walk but don't want to go up the chutes?" I asked.

"All animals fear when they're going to die," he said. "If he don't want to go, if he falls down, they beat him with pipes, kick them, hit them with pieces of wood, stick them with knives. If he still won't move, you wrap the cable around his neck and drag them in with the hoist. You drag them while they're still alive. Choke them to death.

"You've got to have something for whatever situation you're in," he continued. "You can't spend fifteen or twenty minutes on one horse. You have to do whatever you can to get him in that box to get him skinned—fast. You can't let one horse stop you from making money."

An argument flared up on the other side of the room. A guard stood up. The prisoner and his female visitor stopped shouting, crossed their arms over their chests, and looked away from each other. The guard sat back down and yawned.

"See, the thing with a slaughterhouse, every piece of meat is valuable," Parrish said. "Every horse is valuable. Like, a horse that dies out in the pen, maybe he's still warm. By law, that horse is supposed to be condemned, cut up, and incinerated. Instead, we put him in the freezer so the meat can be sold."

The buzzer rang. After the prisoner count, I asked Parrish how the slaughter went for horses who walked to the knocking box.

"There's a certain way to shoot or knock an animal," he said. "I seen them shoot them five times, hit them all in the eye. Hit them in the neck. I seen horses get shot wrong and get right back up and walk around the kill floor, kind of dazed. And they run up on them and just hit them with the knife in the neck, any-where, and just let them suffer, walk around bleeding.

"Sometimes they can't get close enough with the knocking gun," he continued. "It don't work right sometimes, some-times the gun gets wet, gets blood up in it, and it don't shoot. The boss tells us, 'Run and cut his throat.' I've seen my boss grab a knife and run and cut its throat."

"What about the inspector?" I asked. "Does he ever see any of this?"

"Yes."

"How do you know? You've seen him?"

"We all on the kill floor together," he said, "we all watching this. Sometimes he'd complain about it. But you've got a lot of guys there, new, unexperienced, and they think it's a game."

"Do any of the horses regain consciousness after they're hung?"

"Some," he said. "They still be kicking, they still be alive."

"Does anyone ever get hurt?"

"People get their arms broke, get kicked—I got kicked in the nuts. People been bit by them. And they beat the hell out of them. I've seen horses get beat with pipes."

"If the horse is kicking, how do you know it's not just muscle reaction?"

"See, that was my department. I did it so long," he replied. "He'd cry out. Cry and kick. And he'd be choking from the blood, still blowing out air, and I'd start skinning the head."

"How long do they usually have to bleed out?" I asked.

"The sticker and the header is the same person," he said. "You move so fast you don't have time to wait till a horse bleed[s] out. You skin him as he bleeds. Sometimes horses' heads are still down in the blood, sucking up the same blood from some other horse. 'Cause a horse is so long, his nose is down in the blood, blowing bubbles, and he suffocate[s].

"See," he continued, "a job like that, it's a job of cruelty. You don't have no conscience. All you think about is you making your money, you doing your job."

"Sure," I said, "but the USDA's supposed to be enforcing the law."

"But you're moving so fast," he said, "a lot of things slip past. There's times the doc might say, 'I've got to condemn that horse.' Might be part of him's bad, might be the pneumonia's traveled everywhere. I'd drag him back, and my boss would tell me to cut the hindquarters off and bring him into the cooler. This meat's supposed to be condemned, but still you'd cut it up and bag it."

"But don't they have to be stamped 'USDA inspected'?" I asked.

"He got the stamper," he said, "he can stamp it himself after the doc leaves."

"You're saying your boss had access to the USDA stamper?"

"'Course he's got access," he replied. "He's got access to anything in that plant. It's like this: if you a good worker, you

do favors for the boss, he does favors for you. You take a condemned horse, skin him, cut him up, sell the meat in the street.
We have sold horsemeat, unstamped, to people in restaurants,
in their homes. We've sold it as beef. '

"You've done this?" I asked. "Or heard about it from other
people?"

"Heard about it, seen it, done it," he said. "Everybody
want a hustle. I had a buddy who had a key to the plant. He'd
go in and steal horsemeat and sell it in town as beef."

"Didn't people know he worked there? Didn't they think it
was strange that he'd be—"

"Nope," he interrupted, "because they're getting a deal.
He's doing them a favor, helping them save money. You mix
it with beef, cook it right, people don't know the difference. I
could decorate a piece of horsemeat and you'd think it's roast
beef. In restaurants, people eat what you put in front of them."

Parrish looked past me and shouted something I didn't
understand. Someone shouted back at him, and he nodded.

"The USDA man," I said, "did he ever stop the line?"

"If the horses are touching, one getting shit on the other
because the line's clogged up, he'd slow it down a little."

"What about for live animals kicking?"

"Nope," he said. "See, certain guys get an attitude and take
off on the horses. You know, you drink on the job. You go out
to the liquor store on your lunch break and buy your liquor and
beer, and we drink while we work. The USDA peoples drink
with us. Come to our houses and party."

"But that's after work," I said. "Would they drink on the
job?"

"Sure they would. Drink a beer down by the liver stand,
where they check the livers and hearts."

Visiting hours were over. We stood up.

"Can I come see you again tomorrow?" I asked.

He put his arm around my shoulders and gave me a quick squeeze.

"Tomorrow."

*   *   *

The next day when I walked into the prison visiting room, a woman came up to me and introduced herself as BethAnn.

"Steve told me about you," she said. "You came all the way from Washington just to talk to *him*?"

I started to explain my mission, but she didn't seem to be listening.

"Women are always trying to get next to Steve," she was saying. "They find out pretty quick they better not mess with me." A warning with a smile.

BethAnn was squeezed into jeans and a polo shirt a couple of sizes too small. I couldn't quite picture her with Parrish, but you never can tell about these things.

A guard brought Parrish in. He shook my hand, let Beth-Ann kiss his cheek. We sat down. BethAnn fussed over him, asking him about his treatment by the guards and other inmates, his prospects for early release. He told her everything was going just fine.

I didn't want to interview him with BethAnn here. I couldn't just ask her to leave, at least not yet. I asked Parrish if he'd like something to eat from the snack bar.

"Good idea," BethAnn said, and headed on over. Steve and I followed.

BethAnn ordered two burgers, french fries, a piece of pie,

and a Coke. Steve ordered some fries and a Coke. I got a cup of coffee. BethAnn, up ahead at the cashier, said something and pointed to me. I was feeding her out of my limited travel funds?

After BethAnn had finished her meal, Steve leaned close to her and smiled.

"Gail and I got to take care of business now," he said. "See you next time."

After some more fussing over him, she kissed his cheek again, waved to me, and left.

"She started visiting me after I got in here," Steve said. "Didn't know her much but now she come here all the time. Sometimes it happens that way. You, for instance." He was smiling now, pointing back and forth between me and himself. "We understand each other. We could be good together. And here I am, stuck in here. Tell you what—I be getting out in a month. I could come to Washington."

"You and BethAnn?" I asked.

He leaned back in his chair and laughed. "No, just me."

I changed the subject by suggesting that we move out onto the enclosed patio where there was less noise. I asked him about another plant he'd worked in.

"They kill goats, lambs, cattle, and lots of hogs," he said.

"How did they stun the pigs?"

"They had a shocker," he replied. "You're supposed to shock them behind the ear. Problem is, they hit them everywhere. Or hold it on there till it starts smoking and cook the doggone thing. Sometimes they're just cruel to them. They don't get shocked right, they just hang them on the rail, alive and kicking. They stab them and drop them in that water while they still alive. Don't give them no chance for the blood to drain out of them. They rushing so fast," his words came faster and faster, "stick 'em and drop 'em, stick 'em and drop 'em. And they're still alive, still hollering in the water."

"You've personally seen live ones in the scalding tank?" I asked.

"Many times," Steve said. "I actually seen a hog that wasn't stuck right jump out of the tank with the steam still smoking off his body and run through the kill floor. He jumped out and was running around hollering. Not sticking them right and dropping them in the tank alive, that happens at a lot of slaughterhouses. You want some more coffee?"

"I'm fine," I answered. "What about the inspector?"

"The boss used to pay him off in meat, sometimes cash," he said. "To let the hogs go by, to let them get away with killing longer, working overtime. Sometimes the doc would let us take the hogs, the ones that should be condemned. He'd go out to the bar with us.

"People took the bowel system," he continued, "parts that aren't supposed to be sold, and sell them to Chinese restaurants. Tripe and runners and creepers* and nuts. The feet. They sell buckets of blood out the back door. Hog blood, cow blood. They give you a couple of dollars and tell you to fill a bucket with blood for them.

"Another thing, we take iron pipes on baby calves," he said. "Hit them in the head."

"Didn't they have a captive bolt gun?"

"This is faster. 'Cause their skull is still soft. Knock 'em down with a pipe, hang 'em up."

"You know," he continued, "I seen guys take broomsticks

---

*small and large intestines

and stick it up the cow's behind, screwing them with a broom. One time the knocking gun was broke all day, they were taking a knife and cutting the back of the cow's neck open while he's still standing up. They would just fall down and be ashaking. And they stab cows in the butt to make 'em move. Break their tails. They beat them so bad.

"I've drug cows till their bones start breaking, while they were still alive. Bringing them around the corner and they get stuck up in the doorway, just pull them till their hide be ripped, till the blood just drip on the steel and concrete. Breaking their legs pulling them in. And the cow be crying with its tongue stuck out. They pull him till his neck just pop.

"I mean, pulling them cows in with chains and the hoist, breaking their legs, scarring them up, it's, it's like, you know, it's just . . ."

He never got that last word out. We said a brief, subdued good-bye, and I was out of there.

12

A Sixty-Minute Investigation

I had never seen horses being slaughtered before—maybe it was time I did.

I had no contacts at the slaughterhouse I chose nor any way to conduct covert surveillance. I visited the area bars, hoping to meet a plant employee. No luck.

Carol Taylor (my undercover identity) came through for me once again. She went to the plant with a good cover and the owner, a genial man who laughed a lot, welcomed me and talked to me for an hour. Then he had an employee give me a guided tour of the plant. They'd finished killing for the day but answered all my questions. I asked if they'd let me come again to take photographs when they were killing. To my surprise they agreed—smiling.

At six o'clock the next morning I showed up with my

camera. Everyone was on coffee break, but one horse was hanging, another dismembered, and on the floor was a pile of hooves, each with about ten inches of leg attached. I started shooting photos, afraid that if they came back from their break they'd make me stop, if not take my camera. When they did come back, I asked permission to begin shooting, and it was granted. Then the killing started up again.

I documented well-groomed horses as they were prodded into the knocking box, walking with great hesitation in each step. In the first photos, their coats would shine with a healthy luster, their manes carefully groomed. In the next, their blood-stained hides were being peeled from their bodies, their hooves thrown into the pile on the floor. I got shots of foals being herded into the knocking box, skittish at first, then panicked, then lifeless. I just kept shooting.

*   *   *

When I spoke to Mike Wallace's producer from the road, he told me that the executive producer of "60 Minutes" had balked at the idea of airing a story as graphic as the one he had pitched. Still, in spite of the exec's apparent disapproval, the producer told me he'd found an interested ear in his immediate supervisor, Mike Wallace. Wallace, I was told, felt strongly that the violations demanded public attention and he agreed to proceed with the story despite the executive's concerns. Both correspondent and producer felt confident that, once the story was produced, the show's executive producer would realize its merit.

I traveled back to Washington where I met up with Wallace's producer, and provided him with virtually every piece of documentation I had. We agreed to meet in a few weeks in Sioux Falls where we would try to obtain videotape of cattle regaining consciousness at Morrell. The producer, nationally acclaimed for his features, had become deeply committed to the story. But he did inform me that this was the only time he'd ever gone out on a limb to do a story. "Our executive producer is not behind us on this one," he warned, "so nothing better go wrong!"

Over the course of the next few weeks the producer would arrange for camera and soundmen, hotel rooms, and hidden camera equipment. He would squeeze the story into Mike Wallace's busy schedule, book him on a flight, and charter a plane to fly the Morrell employees to Omaha, Nebraska, where everyone—including Mike Hurtsinger, Ed Van Winkle, Tommy Vladak, Clay Calkin, Donny Tice, and Red Martin— would meet for the taping.

In the meantime, I was to fly to Florida to enlist workers to be interviewed on Timothy Walker's behalf. These people would later be flown to New York City where they would also be interviewed by Mike Wallace.

❋   ❋   ❋

When I got to Florida, Kenneth Sardborne, the first USDA brucellosis tester to have corroborated Timothy Walker's claims, showed me a document signed by USDA Regional Director Dr. L. D. Konyha, the same bureaucrat who'd fired Walker. The document, disguised as a "Policy on Answering Questions/Giving Statements," instructed staff not to speak with "individuals unauthorized by the Department" and, when approached by such persons, to contact one's supervisors immediately. The gag order had been issued the day after I'd interviewed Walker's co-worker Ronnie Watson, and made it very clear that speaking with me—whether on duty or off— would be grounds for immediate dismissal.

And an effective gag order it was. Despite their strong desire to come to Walker's defense, none of the brucellosis testers I'd interviewed was willing to sign an affidavit on Walker's behalf. After all, Walker—decorated by the Navy, college-educated, successful in business, respected as a city employee, exemplary as a brucellosis tester—was now jobless, living proof that the USDA would follow through on its threats.

I'd already mailed Gertrude Schneider the translated affi- davits based on the interviews with her "boys," and she'd sent them back signed and notarized by Anna Pedrosa. Hector, Anna's brother, signed his affidavit for me. Billy Corbet, the Kaplan supervisor, agreed to be interviewed on camera, and Albert Cabrera, the knocker, said I was free to use his taped interview in any way I chose.

＊　　＊　　＊

Turbulence en route to Sioux Falls, South Dakota, swatted my 747 all over the sky. Even though the aircraft was violently bouncing about, I found myself experiencing a tremendous sense of relief. I suddenly realized that no longer was the suf- fering of millions of slaughterhouse animals on my shoulders alone. Even if the plane I was traveling in happened to crash, the producer and Mike Wallace now had the documentation, the contacts, and the commitment to break the story to the nation. For the first time in many months, I breathed a sigh of relief.

The plane landed safely in Sioux Falls and an hour later

the producer and I met at a local hotel. I introduced him to a worker—a guy named Paulsen—who would be able to carry the hidden camera equipment unobtrusively and who also had access to the plant's blood pit. While Paulsen was a union official and didn't regularly work in the blood pit, we could only hope that his presence would go unnoticed. Over the next several days, he would spend time visiting the blood pit, socializing with workers, and taping whatever he could get.

Paulsen didn't do much taping that first morning. He felt somewhat conspicuous on the kill floor because he had no legitimate reason to be there, and soon left.

The next day while Paulsen taped, the producer and I waited anxiously at the Labor Temple. During a conversation with another union official, the producer found out that the union was embroiled in a long-term contract dispute with management over wages, and he began to look nervous.

Paulsen had taped for less than an hour that day and got few live cows, only one of which was obviously and undeniably conscious. Despite the limited time he had taped, the producer, apparently terrified of a lawsuit and anxious about having gone against the wishes of his executive producer, jumped to the conclusion that the employees' charges were trumped up to smear the company's name. He proceeded to cancel all preparations for the story—the interviews, the chartered plane, Mike Wallace's inbound flight. As I struggled to hold back my tears, he quickly booked the next available flight out of Sioux Falls and was on his way home.

That afternoon, Bucky White came in the Labor Temple, waved, got himself a cup of coffee, and then sat down next to me.

"Don't know about you, but I'm having a great week," Bucky said. "No live beef in the stick pit for two whole days."

"How come?"

"Knocking gun air pressure's turned way up," he said.

Chris O'Day joined us and clinked coffee cups with White.

"Quiet day at the ranch, huh?"

"Why's the knocker's air pressure up?" I asked.

Chris laughed and said, "You know how Paulsen's been in there a lot?" White nodded.

"The foreman said Paulsen was doing a safety report or something," she continued, "so he cranked the air pressure way up."

I dove for the pay phone on the wall and tried to get word to the producer, but his flight had already left. Then I called his assistant back in Manhattan.

"About the Sioux Falls story," I said, "have your boss call me the second he gets off the plane."

"Story's been scratched."

"I found out what went wrong. Management—"

"The story's scratched."

"But he doesn't know—"

"I talked to him," he interrupted. "He doesn't care what happened. The story's scratched, canceled, called off, null and void, dead."

PART FOUR

USDA DEREGULATES: FULL LINE SPEEDS AHEAD

13

A Pandora's Box
of Pathogens

We used to trim the shit off the meat.
Then we washed the shit off the meat.
Now the consumer eats the shit off the meat.
                                    —David Carney
                                    USDA Meat Inspector

"Kevin's favorite hug was a group hug," said Holly Scott, a small, young woman with blonde hair and a soft, high-pitched voice. She was testifying at yet another congressional briefing on meat inspection, held in February 1995, and I was attending. "Kevin, Mom, and Dad would encircle with a heartfelt hug around their necks," she continued. "Kevin was a miracle child, because I had major health problems which were complicated by pregnancy. It was very risky to become pregnant; I had to be hospitalized nearly every six weeks."

"It's been over a year now since we have had one of these group hugs from Kevin; or, for that matter, any contact with Kevin." Kevin's mom and grandmom had taken Kevin to the mall to have his portrait shot. He was rewarded for being a good boy for the photographer with a fast-food lunch. "Kevin insisted on having a 'hanabur wis cheese on it' that day. The photo I have is a bittersweet reminder of that day. Bitter because just minutes later he took about four bites of food that would end his life. Sweet because it is one of the last images we have of Kevin." Over the next few weeks, Kevin's body was slowly dismantled, organ by organ.

"The last story I read to Kevin was his favorite bedtime story, *Good Night Moon*. The pages read, 'Good night stars, good night air. Good night noises everywhere.' The next day, Kevin's heart stopped beating. He went to sleep forever."

And thus, Kevin, the only child that Holly Scott would ever have, became just another statistic. He was one of an estimated five hundred victims who now die each year in the United States from E. coli 0157:H7 poisoning. E. coli 0157:H7, known to contaminate meat during sloppy, high-speed slaughter operations, generally takes with it the most vulnerable victims: children and the elderly.

✻   ✻   ✻

Now back in Washington from Sioux Falls, I contacted an Emmy Award–winning producer I knew at ABC's news magazine "20/20." My brief description of the investigation and the piles of evidence I had so far amassed intrigued him; he was convinced the story had the makings of a powerful exposé. I sent him all the materials I had transcribed, and he prepared to pitch the story to his boss, the show's executive producer. Ultimately, he felt that he'd have a better chance of selling the story to his boss if he pitched the human-impact angle. So I sent him some information I'd collected from the Government Accountability Project (GAP) suggesting a link between increased line speeds and meat contamination. Still, as much as he wanted to do the story, his boss patently rejected the idea.

Next, I contacted a producer at ABC's "PrimeTime Live." I wrote a lengthy explanation of the case for her, then worked with her and a second producer for several weeks. Again, as much as they wanted to run with the story, both women were concerned that it was too graphic for program executives' tastes.

"PrimeTime," meanwhile, was working on a related story which ended up running instead of mine. It concentrated on the increasingly serious problem of meat contamination. It was an important, effective show and used some of the material I'd sent the producers, but it didn t touch on the subject of animal abuse.

With "PrimeTime" I confronted some hard truths about my fight. While I'd been trying to publicize the suffering of animals, "20/20" had asked me for stories about how slaughterhouse abuses affected people, and "PrimeTime" aired a show about consumer hazards. While I'd been focused on the welfare of animals and workers, there was yet another issue that I needed to explore further.

It was time for me to catch up.

᠅   ᠅   ᠅

I called the U.S. Centers for Disease Control and Prevention (CDC) in Atlanta to get more information about the hazards of contaminated meat. According to the CDC, foodborne illness is one of the nation's most preventable public health hazards. Yet, after looking at the statistics they sent, it became clear that food-poisoning deaths had climbed dramatically since the USDA began relaxing meat inspection procedures and standards in the 1980s. As the meat packing industry had become increasingly consolidated during the Reagan and Bush administrations, line speeds had skyrocketed and so, too, had the number of cases of foodborne illness.

The CDC calculates that between 6.5 and 81 million cases of food poisoning occur each year in the United States: that is, as many as one out of every three Americans suffers a food-borne illness each year. While most sufferers experience flu-like symptoms—diarrhea and vomiting—roughly half a million of those cases require hospitalization. Deaths from food poisoning more than quadrupled during the decade of deregulation from an estimated two thousand in 1984 to roughly nine thousand in 1994. The major source of these infections is foods of animal origin.*

The CDC estimates that there are now 40,000 cases of E. coli 0157:H7 poisoning every year. And even that figure may be underestimated. Not all states require doctors to notify health authorities of incidents of E. coli 0157 poisoning. And many doctors, hospitals, and laboratories don't yet know to test for E. coli 0157.

Most deaths from E. coli or salmonella are erroneously

*Other infective agents include produce and water (often contaminated by manure from cattle, sheep, other animals).

ascribed to other ailments like cardiac or pulmonary arrest or stroke, the secondary illnesses that result from bacterial invasion. Infection by foodborne pathogens rarely shows up on death certificates, which also dramatically limits reporting to the CDC.

While poultry has long had the reputation as the leading carrier of foodborne illness, not only sickening and killing, but causing chronic disabilities like arthritis, it's the E. coli outbreaks that have been generating the most attention lately.

With one hamburger containing meat from as many as one hundred different animals, one infected animal can cross-contaminate sixteen tons of beef. And because the grinding process creates a much larger surface area for the bacteria to inhabit than a cut of beef, they find hamburger meat especially hospitable.

According to the CDC, in 1986, E. coli 0157:H7 infected thirty-seven Washington State residents, sent seventeen to the hospital, and took the lives of two elderly women after they ate contaminated beef in a fast-food restaurant. The following year, fifty-one people at a Utah mental institution contracted "hamburger disease," as it is now called; eight were hospitalized, and four died. A year later, sixty-one Wisconsin schoolchildren got sick from eating USDA-approved roast beef, and another fifty-four Minnesota students were infected after eating precooked hamburger patties. In 1990, sixty North Dakotans and ten Montana schoolchildren were infected with the bug.

It wasn't until 1993, however, when more than seven hundred people got sick enough to need medical help after eating undercooked hamburgers at a Seattle Jack-in-the-Box fast-food restaurant, that E. coli began to make headlines. Scores of area residents were hospitalized, fifty-six developed HUS (hemolytic uremic syndrome), and three young children died.

Another one hundred and six people who ate at Jack-in-the-Box restaurants in Idaho, California, and Nevada subsequently contracted symptoms of E. coli poisoning, and one died.

That same year, while reporting methods changed slightly, the CDC recorded twenty-one major outbreaks of E. coli 0157:H7—more than the *combined* total of outbreaks reported in the bacterium's entire eleven-year history.

In 1994 and 1995, a total of sixty-five U.S. outbreaks were reported to the CDC. In 1996, STOP statistics included: church-goers in Minnesota who were sickened at a roast beef supper, a New Jersey boy dead from a hamburger, eighteen people in New Hampshire ill from ground beef purchased at supermarkets, a group of Indiana children infected in a school lunch program, and seventy people at a work picnic in Montana. In 1997, in just one of many outbreaks, Hudson Foods meat-processing plant in Nebraska was forced to recall 25 million pounds of potentially contaminated ground beef—until that time the biggest meat recall in history—after seventeen Colorado residents were infected with E. coli 0157:H7.*

I phoned Tom Devine, legal director of the Government Accountability Project (GAP), for his opinion on the rash of outbreaks. "The primary advice USDA offered in response to the Jack-in-the-Box tragedy," he said, "was that consumers are proceeding at their own risk if they eat rare or medium beef.

---

*In December 1998, a 22-state outbreak of the deadly pathogen Listeria monocytogenes initiated a recall of 35 million pounds of hot dogs and lunch meat manufactured by a Sara Lee plant in Michigan. The outbreak caused 15 deaths, six miscarriages, and 100 illnesses, all attributed to contaminated product manufactured at that plant. Also in 1998: according to the CDC, the number of E.coli 0157:H7 outbreaks jumped 50 percent from 1997.

Like other segments of the livestock industry, ranchers and feedlot operators are producing ever more meat for a dramatically expanding global market. Between 1985 and 1995, U.S. beef exports rose 450 percent. U.S. pork exports increased 500 percent and poultry exports climbed 800 percent, as well. World food demand is expected to double due to population growth and rising incomes by the year 2020. (USDA photo)

Veal calves are chained at the neck inside wooden crates for their entire lives. They can not walk, or even turn around. Fed an anemia-inducing liquid diet, veal calves require the continuous administration of antibiotics and other drugs just to keep them alive. During her slaughterhouse investigation, the author documented the presence of clenbuterol–a toxic, steroidlike drug smuggled into the United States to speed growth in calves–in more than one-third of the samples she collected. (Author's photo)

At any given time, roughly 243 million laying hens—nearly one bird for every man, woman, and child in the United States—are living in cramped cages like the ones pictured here. Crowded together and living on sloping wire which cuts into their feet, hens can neither stretch their wings, preen, nor sit comfortably when laying their eggs. Thousands of hens, like the bird at the far left (bottom of front cage), are trampled to death by cagemates each day. For every egg consumed in this country, a hen will have lived 26 hours under conditions like these. (Author's photo)

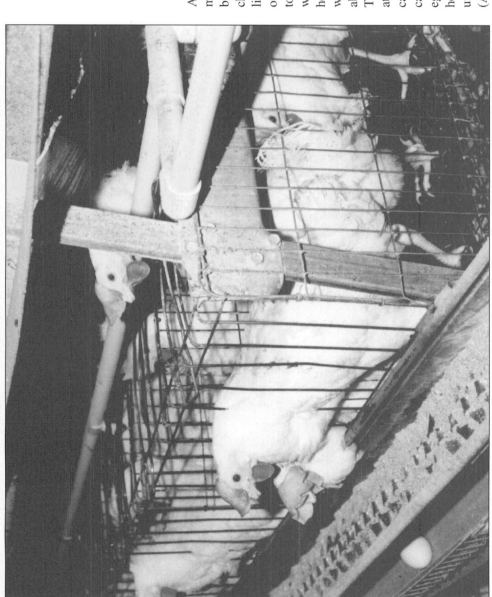

Millions of female breeding hogs spend years confined inside metal crates so small that they can not walk or even turn around. Forced to live, eat, sleep, and give birth on concrete or metal flooring, inhaling the fumes of their own waste, sows develop severe respiratory and leg problems. As a result, thousands collapse and ultimately have to be dragged from their crates. (Author's photo)

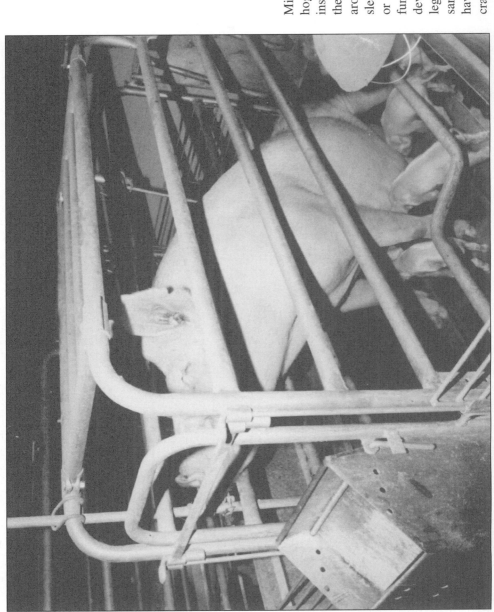

The poultry industry currently slaughters more chickens in one day than it did in *the entire year* of 1930. Expedient production practices, skyrocketing line speeds, and reduced federal oversight are largely responsible for a dramatic increase in microbial contamination of birds and in the corresponding rise in foodborne illness in humans. (USDA photo)

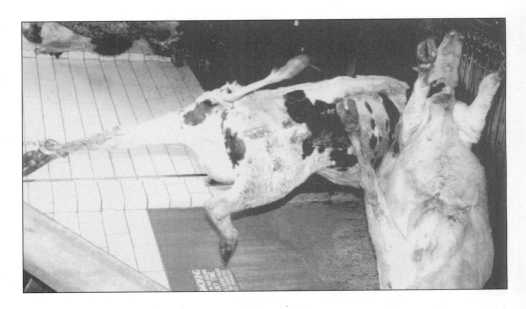

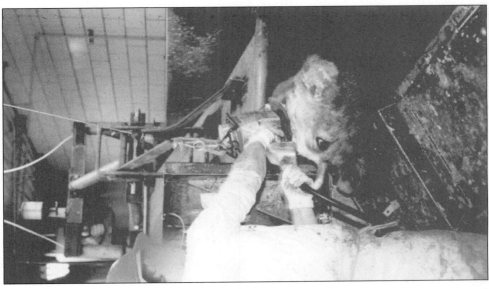

According to the Humane Slaughter Act, all animals are supposed to be rendered insensible to pain prior to being shackled, hoisted, and bled. That federal law, however, is rarely enforced. **(Right)** A worker uses an air-powered knocking gun intended to render a cow unconscious. **(Far Right)** An animal is hoisted up on to the moving overhead rail and transported to the sticker for throat cutting. If the knocking gun is not properly serviced or the stun operator is not properly trained, the cow may go through much of the slaughter process conscious. (Author's photos)

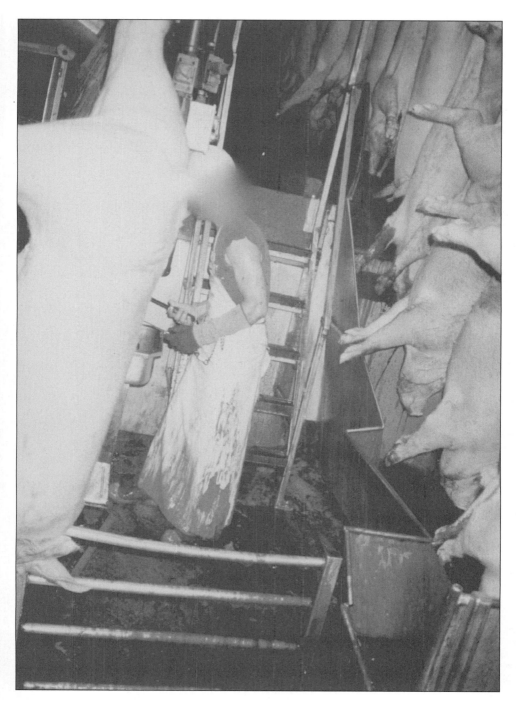

With huge corporate packing plants putting thousands of smaller operations out of business, slaughter line speeds have soared. A hog "sticker" may cut the throats of as many as 1,100 hogs an hour—or nearly one hog every three seconds. With line speeds this fast, workers often resort to brutality to keep the production line running to keep from losing their jobs. (Author's photo)

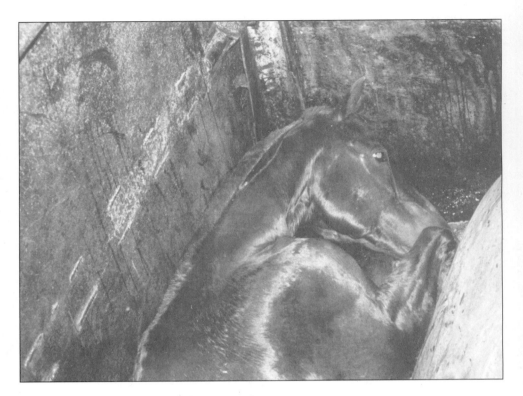

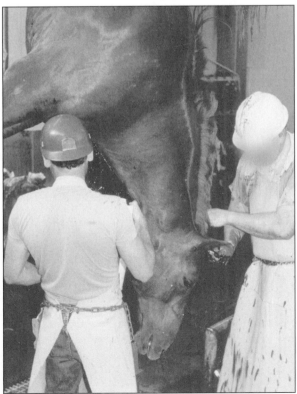

Each year in the United States, hundreds of thousands of horses are slaughtered for human consumption. **(Above)** This horse, a former companion animal, has been shot with a captive bolt gun and has collapsed inside the knocking box. **(Left)** A horse has been stunned and stuck, and workers are skinning out the animal's head. The meat from these animals will be shipped overseas. (Author's photos)

Twenty years ago, Gail, it wasn't a reckless, foolhardy act for a family to eat medium-rare hamburgers or steak for Sunday dinner. Something has drastically changed if the USDA is warning people that federally approved beef has to be cooked to a crisp in order to avoid food poisoning tragedies. So, what's changed?" he asked. "Obviously, the meat's a lot dirtier."

By now I was swimming in documents. My dining room table was hidden beneath stacks of files. But I still wanted to know more about meat inspection procedures.

I learned that about six thousand federal meat inspectors examined the insides and outsides of more than eight billion animals each year. Meat inspectors had been using the same methods for nearly ninety years—cutting into, manually examining, and visually observing carcasses and organs—relying solely on their senses of sight, smell, and touch to examine the animals for signs of disease and contamination.

As early as 1985, the National Academy of Sciences (NAS) had warned the USDA to take immediate action to stem the tide of contamination that was sure to hit. That year, the NAS issued the first of three separate reports analyzing the nation's meat and poultry inspection systems, calling them antiquated in their ability to protect the public, and urging the USDA to begin designing a science-based inspection system to detect lethal pathogens—disease-causing organisms—invisible to the naked eye. According to the NAS, contaminants like E. coli and salmonella exposed consumers to a whole new world of food hazards, and posed a significantly greater threat than did diseases that could be seen, smelled, or felt.

"It is virtually impossible to detect these organisms with current inspection methods," the NAS warned. Furthermore, the NAS stated that it could find "no clear evidence that the

[USDA's] inspection program [was even] based on objectives and criteria that relate to public health."

"We hurried to finish the report," one NAS committee member said. "We felt a sense of urgency. We thought our recommendations were going to be implemented."

As bacterial outbreaks continued to rise, all three NAS reports strongly advised the USDA to begin developing rapid in-plant screening tests for microscopic contaminants—tests that could get results in minutes rather than the several days that currently available testing methods were taking. While inspectors would continue to conduct visual exams for signs of pathology and gross contamination, microbial screening would also enable them to test for microscopic pathogens.*

When the USDA looked to the NAS for recommendations—the USDA itself had commissioned the studies—microbial testing was not the solution the agency wanted to hear. Despite the fact that the death toll had already begun to rise of consumers who had eaten meat and poultry labeled "wholesome," and new, hardier strains of bacteria were beginning to emerge, the USDA failed to incorporate most of the NAS's recommendations into its inspection procedures.

Instead, USDA officials implemented their own "modernization" program for the twenty-first century; one that not only reduced the number of inspectors and relaxed standards for

---

*The NAS also recommended the use of animal traceback systems to determine the sources of diseased and contaminated animals, the identification and monitoring of potential points of contamination in the production, slaughter, and distribution processes, and the use of sampling to verify product wholesomeness. The NAS strongly warned "against the use of samples if simply to reduce the total inspection effort with current methods."

wholesomeness in the nation's largest slaughterhouses, but actually turned over its authority for controlling microbial contamination to the packing plants themselves. By washing their hands of contamination control and deputizing the plants to police themselves, USDA officials stated that they could continue to guarantee the wholesomeness of America's food supply, while enabling plants to boost productivity by as much as 40 percent.

* * *

My doctor had told me to take it easy and reduce the stress in my life. Friends told me to take some time off and stop working so hard. I headed out of Washington, D.C., for Maryland's Eastern Shore and a day at the beach.

Maryland's Eastern Shore is also a major poultry-producing region. I was all too familiar with red-meat operations but not with the poultry industry, where the deregulation of the 1980s had first started. As long as I was passing through, there seemed no good reason not to stop and have a look at a chicken farm.

The "farm" I noticed close to the highway was a warehouse the size of a football field. I pulled off for a closer look. Its huge doors were open for ventilation with giant screens keeping the "broilers"—chickens raised for meat—inside. A young couple came out of the nearby farmhouse. They agreed to show me around.

Inside, the air was thick with ammonia and dust. Through watering, stinging eyes I saw what I'd only seen in textbook photos: a sea of forty thousand chickens packed together so tightly in one giant shed they could hardly move, pecking around in their own droppings on the floor.

I'd read that big operations like this produce on average

about five hundred pounds of dead birds each day. So I wasn't surprised when I noticed that here and there a chicken was lying on its back, motionless. When I pointed to one and asked the grower about it, he said it had died of "flip-over disease." It used to take four months to grow a three-pound bird, he explained, and now, thanks to genetics and growth stimulants, it took only six weeks. That was more than their bodies could handle, he said, and so they flipped over, dead from a heart attack at the ripe old age of one month.

Behind the warehouse a huge pile of dead birds swarmed with flies, filling the air with the smell of rot.

I didn't make it to the beach that day.

※   ※   ※

Next I visited an egg factory. This also looked nothing like a traditional farm. Inside the three huge warehouses were rows of cages four tiers high. These buildings housed 375,000 birds, crammed four to a cage with floor space measuring a foot by a foot and a half.

Living on sloping wire floors, so that the eggs roll out to a conveyor belt, with the wire cutting into their feet, the hens' legs were deformed and their feet covered with blisters and sores. I remembered seeing a demonstration where a battery (caged) hen was released and placed on solid ground. The bird was so crippled, she couldn't even stand.

As is typical throughout the egg industry, the birds at this operation couldn't stretch their wings or even sit comfortably to lay their eggs. Watching them struggle for cage space, it became clear why hatchery workers sear off chicks' beaks— they would resort to anything to prevent birds kept under these conditions from pecking each other to death. As it was, many of the birds were raw and bloody and had few feathers left. And, because the worker who picks the dead hens out of the cages hadn't yet made his morning rounds, birds that had been flattened—trampled to death by their cell mates—were still littering the floors of their cages.*

✻   ✻   ✻

At the time of my visit to these operations, the poultry industry was slaughtering more birds in one day than it had in the entire year of 1930. How did they kill so many animals so quickly? The USDA was happy to provide me with statistics, charts, and pamphlets showing how poultry slaughterhouses run—at least, how they are supposed to run, or how we are supposed to think they run. GAP's whistleblower files fleshed out the theoretical with accounts of the actual.

Once dumped from their cages and shackled upside down to an overhead conveyor, chickens begin their journey through

---

*After a year of producing nearly an egg a day, the survivors are gassed or ground up alive to be fed back to other chickens; slaughtered for use in the school lunch program or in pet food, says *Feedstuffs,* an industry trade magazine; or "recycled" to spend to another laying cycle in the crowded cages. To shorten the hens' natural resting period between laying cycles, farmers deprive "recycled" birds of *all* food for from five to fifteen days. The practice, called forced molting, shocks the hens into abruptly shedding their feathers, and hastens the beginning of a new and simultaneous laying cycle. During this process, about a third of the birds die from starvation and acute stress. The fate of the emaciated survivors: another laying cycle in the battery cage.

the nation's slaughterhouses—twenty-five to thirty million of them every *day*.

Since it's easier to bleed a bird that isn't flapping and struggling, most live birds have their heads dragged through an electrically charged water bath to paralyze—not stun—them. Other industrialized nations require that chickens be rendered unconscious or killed prior to bleeding and scalding, so they won't have to go through those processes conscious.* Here in the United States, however, poultry plants—exempt from the Humane Slaughter Act and still clinging to the industry myth that a dead animal won't bleed properly—keep the stunning current down to about one-tenth of that needed to render a chicken unconscious.†

A conveyor then carries the shocked and paralyzed birds to a high-speed circular blade meant to slit their throats but which occasionally misses birds as they rush past at the rate of thousands per hour. After about a minute's bleed-out, the birds are dunked into a scald tank to loosen their feathers, then run through a series of machines with thousands of rubberized "fingers" that literally beat the feathers off their bodies.

After their heads and feet are removed and they've been

---

*In the 1980s, European researchers demonstrated that, on average, only about one-third of supposedly stunned birds leaving the electrically charged water bath were properly stunned. As a result of this and subsequent research, England and other member nations of the European Union have increased stunning amperages dramatically to ensure that birds are killed by electrocution prior to bleeding and scalding.

†The nation's 261 million laying hens are neither rendered unconscious nor paralyzed. After a year or more of laying eggs, their bones are so brittle that immersion in an electrically charged water bath would cause them to shatter.

washed, the chickens are rehung on an evisceration line. There, machines automatically cut them open and pull their guts out. After examination by a USDA inspector, it's off to the chill tank, a giant refrigerated vat of water where up to six thousand birds are communally cooled for processing. Today, thanks to automation in the industry, individual poultry plants operating in this fashion can kill and process as many as 500,000 birds per day.

The technological innovations of the 1970s that made high-speed, high-volume poultry slaughter possible—all of which were approved by the USDA—are also largely responsible for a dramatic increase in contaminated birds in these plants. In the scald tank, fecal contamination on skin and feathers gets inhaled by live birds, and hot water opens birds' pores allowing pathogens to seep in. The pounding action of the defeathering machines creates an aerosol of feces-contaminated water which is then beaten into the birds. Contamination also occurs when the birds have their intestines removed by automatic eviscerating machines. The high-speed machines commonly rip open intestines, spilling feces into the birds' body cavities.

Prior to 1978, USDA inspectors had to condemn any bird with fecal contamination inside its body cavity. In 1978, citing the problem with the automatic eviscerators, the poultry industry convinced the USDA to reclassify feces from a dangerous contaminant to a "cosmetic blemish" and allow workers simply to rinse it off. The result: inspectors began condemning half as many birds. Consumers ate the rest.

The new industry-wide practice of washing feces-contaminated birds, billed as a "sanitation reform," makes birds look wholesome but does little more than embed bacteria more deeply into the animals' tissues. Since 1978, USDA scientists have learned that rinsing a chicken as many as forty times does not remove all the bacteria. Thanks to the USDA's acquiescence to an industry demand, the department's approval of washing poultry would prove to open the floodgates to an uncontrollable sea of contamination.

Another example of high-speed contamination occurs when the chickens are immersed in the chill tank. "Water in these tanks has been aptly named 'fecal soup' for all the filth and bacteria floating around," GAP's Tom Devine told me. "By immersing clean, healthy birds in the same tank with dirty ones, you're practically assuring cross-contamination. Chickens that bathe together get contaminated together."

While European and Canadian poultry processors use air-chilling systems which reduce the risk of contamination, the U.S. poultry industry's reliance on water chilling has remained strong—and for good reason. Federal regulations permit each carcass to soak up water—until 1997, as much as 8 percent water—during the chilling process. This in effect enables the industry to sell hundreds of millions of gallons of germ-filled water at poultry-meat prices. U.S. poultry consumers spend more than $1 billion on added water per year.*

"With the advent of modern slaughter technologies," said

---

*The red meat industry, envious of the poultry industry's ability to sell water at meat prices, filed a lawsuit in 1994 against the USDA. (Retained water in beef carcasses is deemed a form of adulteration.) In July 1997, a federal judge ruled that the 8 percent water retention allowance in poultry was "arbitrary and capricious." The USDA is currently considering a proposal that will set a 5 percent water retention standard for both poultry *and red meat.*

former USDA microbiologist Gerald Kuester, "there are about fifty points during processing where cross-contamination can occur. At the end of the line, the birds are no cleaner than if they had been dipped in a toilet."

******

Until the early 1980s, USDA inspectors not only carefully examined each bird for a long list of diseases and condemned those with pathological conditions, they were also responsible for ensuring the removal of contaminants like feces and partially digested food. "Trimmable conditions" that didn't affect the entire carcass—broken legs, bruises, blisters, scabs, and sores—had to be cut away.

When such defects were found on a bird, the inspector pointed them out to a plant worker, oversaw their removal, and then reinspected the finished product to make sure it complied with stringent inspection standards. If he had to stop the production line to ensure compliance, he stopped the line. It was the inspectors' authority to check for contaminants, stop production, and reexamine the product that restricted the speed at which the line could run.

As if the filth-producing technologies of the late 1970s hadn't already made poultry dangerous enough, when the Reagan administration came into office, the USDA decided the time had come to deregulate. Agency appointees reasoned that by "streamlining" the inspection process by forcing inspectors to concentrate on disease detection alone, inspectors would no longer be stopping the line for a long list of contaminants. By turning contamination control over to company employees—who could be intimidated or fired at will—and by allowing an increased number of "defects"—feces, scabs, inflammations, bruises, blisters—to pass freely into human food channels, the USDA could cut its inspection force and let the poultry industry run its plants at full throttle. In 1983, Streamlined Inspection was formally proposed and implemented as a pilot in some plants.

"Streamlined Inspection didn't formally affect line speeds," said GAP's Tom Devine. "Rather, at these plants inspectors were stripped of their ability to detect conditions that would justify stopping the line." By removing the greatest obstacle to production—the inspectors' authority—USDA officials could enable the pilot plants to double and even triple their line speeds.

By 1985, when Streamlined Inspection was implemented in poultry plants nationwide, 450 fewer USDA poultry inspectors were examining a billion and a half more birds than ten years earlier. Inspectors who in the 1960s had examined eighteen birds per minute were now required to inspect up to thirty-five birds per minute—fifteen thousand a day. They were provided roughly one and a half seconds to examine each bird inside and out—theoretically inspecting both the carcass and viscera* for twelve different diseases and a host of abnormalities.

Without authority over contamination, inspectors could no longer reinspect feces-covered chickens at the end of the line. When they came across "trimmable conditions" such as lesions or broken bones, they were no longer permitted to oversee the trimming process. And while in theory poultry inspectors could still condemn diseased birds, the new regulations prevented them from ensuring that condemned birds were actually taken off the line.

---

*Viscera are the organs inside the carcass.

To give the appearance of federal oversight, however, inspectors were granted the authority to sample birds at the end of the line. They were permitted to sample ten birds per fifteen thousand slaughtered, less than one-tenth of 1 percent, hardly a statistically valid sample.

❋   ❋   ❋

I'd read the official reports from the government agencies, now I needed to hear what the men and women in the plants had to say. I phoned a veteran USDA poultry inspector, a friend of a friend.

"At my last plant," he said, "birds were going by me at a rate of ninety-one per minute, with three inspectors on the line. There's no way in the world you can look at thirty or thirty-five birds in one minute. About all you can do with birds going past that fast is to pat each one on the behind as it whizzes by."

For a highly acclaimed series that ran in the *Atlanta Journal Constitution,* reporter Scott Bronstein conducted interviews with eighty-four USDA poultry inspectors from thirty-seven plants, many of whom voiced the extreme frustration they experienced in trying to enforce the law. Every week, Bronstein wrote, millions of chickens "leaking yellow pus, stained by green feces, contaminated by harmful bacteria, or marred by lung and heart infections, cancerous tumors, or skin conditions are shipped for sale to consumers."

In addition, GAP obtained affidavits from many poultry workers and inspectors documenting the conditions in their plants. Former Perdue worker Donna Bazemore twice submitted testimony to Congress on conditions in poultry plants. "The plants are filthy," she reported in her first testimony:

> The floors are covered with grease, fat, sand, and roaches. Bugs are up and down the sides of the walls. Some of the flying roaches were huge, up to four and five inches long. We'd joke that you could put a collar on them and walk them. . . . There are flies all around, including big blowflies. Employees are constantly chewing and spitting out snuff and tobacco on the floor.
>
> There is so much fecal contamination on the floor from chickens that it kept getting into one worker's boots and burned his feet so badly his toenails had to be amputated.
>
> The waste is not always from the chickens. The company won't allow workers to leave the line when they have to go to the bathroom. . . . Usually they just suffer and put a strain on their bodies, but sometimes they have to relieve themselves on the floor.
>
> The problems are just as bad in the slaughter process [as they are in the plants generally]. After they are hung, sometimes the chickens fall off into the drain that runs down the middle of the line. This is where roaches, intestines, diseased parts, fecal contamination, and blood are washed down. Workers get sick to their stomachs into the drain. The drain is a lot less sanitary than anybody's toilet. That doesn't seem to matter, though. The Perdue supervisors told us to take the fallen chickens out of the drain and send them back down the line.

Perdue repudiated Bazemore's allegations. The USDA conducted an "investigation" and then issued a statement saying they'd found "no evidence of the kind of gross violations" Bazemore had reported.

Shortly thereafter, a former Perdue worker and two USDA inspectors submitted affidavits of their own to GAP.

"Ms. Bazemore is right about the unsanitary working conditions," the former worker reported.

> While on the night shift, I often saw roaches crawling up and down the walls, as well as flies and mosquitoes. I've seen birds fall on the floor and foremen tell workers to put them back on the line without washing. And I know we didn't condemn those that fell on the floor and were heavily soiled.
>
> I've seen birds with cancerous tumors come through regularly, sometimes all day long. While on quality control, I'd pull off those I saw, but I couldn't possibly catch them all. Right after I'd put them in the condemn barrel, foremen would have the floor workers hang the birds back on the line.

One of the USDA inspectors said he'd "estimate the cockroaches were up to four inches long. One time we shined a flashlight into a hole in the wall where they were crawling in and out, and they were so thick it was like maggots, you couldn't even see a surface."

The other inspector testified:

> Anyone reading this may wonder why the inspectors didn't do something to stop the problems. The leadership at the Department of Agriculture wouldn't let us. . . . The way the agency changed the standards, "modern" means "dirty."
>
> We used to stop production for hours if necessary to get the facility cleaned up. But by the time I left, anyone who tried to do that would have to find another job. The supervisors almost always overruled any inspector who got in the

way, and I kept getting warned not to do it again. Finally, I
stopped enforcing the law and started just following orders.

Two years after Bazemore's first testimony to Congress,
she submitted an update:

> Workers keep finding rats and fat cockroaches in the chill
> tanks where chickens soak together—both the rats and
> their droppings. Women still keep having to relieve them-
> selves on the floor because there are not enough bathroom
> breaks. Birds still fall onto the floor and are put back on
> the line. If the USDA catches the worker doing it, Perdue
> scapegoats the employee. But employees are in trouble if
> they don't try to slip the chickens back in. Chickens keep
> getting removed from the condemn barrel and slipped past
> USDA. Gall birds [chickens with ruptured gall bladders]
> keep going out despite green pus in their intestines that is
> intensely painful when it gets in workers' eyes. Diseased
> birds still go out although they are so sick that mucus
> backs up into their lungs.

A recent GAP investigation into conditions in six poultry
plants in North Carolina turned up similar conditions.

"There were lots of rats, snakes, cockroaches, and maggots
in the plant," one worker said. "I saw flies on the chicken as it
went down the line and maggots in boxes which contained
bags that the chicken would be wrapped in."

A worker at another plant described the chicken processed
at the plant as "not safe to eat. Every day, I saw black chicken,
green chicken, chicken that stank, and chicken with feces on
it. Chicken like this is supposed to be thrown away, but instead
it would be sent down the line to be processed."

An employee at a third plant said, "I personally have seen rotten meat—you can tell by the odor. This rotten meat is mixed with fresh meat and sold for baby food. We are asked to mix it with the fresh food, and this is the way it is sold. You can see the worms inside the meat."

One employee told a USDA inspector that "hundreds of maggots were in the clothes hamper where our smocks were kept." Another worker, "in the department where chicken bones were ground up and processed into chicken franks and bologna," reported that "almost continuously, the bones had an awful, foul odor. Sometimes they came from other plants and had been sitting for days. Often there were maggots on them. These bones were never cleaned off and so the maggots were ground up with everything else and remained in the final product."

✳   ✳   ✳

While the USDA officially reports that 20 percent of all raw chickens are tainted with salmonella, USDA studies from the late 1980s until the present prove otherwise. One of the earliest studies, conducted at a model poultry operation in Puerto Rico in 1987, put the number of contaminated birds coming out of the chill tank at 76 percent. When the study was repeated, the figure was 80 percent. USDA studies conducted in 1992 at five plants in the Southeast found salmonella contamination levels averaging 58 percent before the chickens went into the chill tank, and 72 percent after the communal bath.

Former USDA microbiologist Dr. Gerald Kuester, who was a member of the team conducting the Puerto Rico study, was assigned to publish papers summarizing the findings.

"Clearly, my draft article was not what the agency wanted me to produce," Kuester later said in testimony submitted in Congress. He alleged that his supervisor directed him to change the paper's content precisely where its data would have most effectively warned the public about salmonella contamination.

"I refused to do that," he said. "The agency subsequently proposed my termination for unacceptable performance and eventually published a sanitized version of the article."

Kuester resigned before he could be fired, and accused the agency of having rushed into the Puerto Rico study in an effort to justify "a policy that already had been made to further relax poultry inspection." The USDA, he said in his affidavit, had developed previous regulatory policies in a "vacuum of scientific research," failed to check the public-health impact of new technologies that drastically increased contamination levels, and used skewed testing methods to produce planned results.

To combat the excessive contamination caused by increased line speeds and new technologies, elevated levels of chlorine are added to chill water, a controversial solution because it causes the formation of toxic by-products associated with increased cancer risk in humans. "The 'decontamination' of poultry is not allowed in the European Union (EU)," states a 1997 EU press release in regard to the United States's use of chlorine. "If contamination occurs, EU legislation requires that the part must be removed by the meat inspector."

Here in the United States, despite the use of chlorine, changes in the configuration of the scald tank, on-line rinses and sprays, and other so-called improvements, scalding and chill-tank water continues to cross-contaminate birds. One study examining the impact of six different poultry-processing improvements determined that even with all six modifications in place, salmonella contaminated up to 48 percent of the birds coming out of the chill tank.

Another bacterium called Campylobacter, which occurs twice as frequently as salmonella, has a relatively high occurrence in young adults, and is now the number-one cause of gastroenteritis in the United States, causing hundreds of deaths each year. In 1991, a USDA microbiologist and leading authority on Campylobacter found the bacteria present in 98 percent of store-bought chickens. According to the National Academy of Sciences, studies of market-ready chickens found Campylobacter on up to 82 percent. And in a survey of fifty brand-name broilers in Georgia, a government researcher found 90 percent contaminated with Campylobacter.

Even *Food Safety Review,* the USDA's own publication, reported that "heavily contaminated flocks may result in a contamination rate of 100 percent for finished products." And again, even with chlorine and the other "improvements" in place, Campylobacter was found on up to 100 percent of the chickens coming out of the chill tank.

14

The USDA's Sacred Cow

Once Streamlined Poultry Inspection proved itself a boon to
industry profits, USDA appointees declared it a success and
expanded the program to cattle slaughter. They picked as
pilot locations five of the country's largest beef plants,
whose operations accounted for roughly 20 percent of the
beef produced in the United States. In these plants, they cut
the number of inspectors and abolished the final carcass
inspection station, where inspectors used to watch for contaminants such as feces, hair, dirt, and grease. The law still
required contaminants to be cut away but, according to GAP,
company quality-control workers who replaced USDA
inspectors rarely visited the line. Under strict orders from
management to see that meat remained untrimmed—trimming reduces carcass weight and cuts into profits—they

were subject to demotion or dismissal if they interfered with production in any way.

Instead, if contamination was to be removed, it would have to happen during the cosmetic rinsing that was supposed to take place after trimming to make the finished carcass look nice. Read one inspector's affidavit: "Inspectors call the washing operation a 'shit spreader.' It's a way to make the cross-contamination worse."

Product standards were reduced over the course of the pilot program to the lowest common denominator that the plants thought they could meet. For example, five specks of feces were considered one defect, while four specks represented none. Four hairs were no longer a defect, but fourteen hairs counted as one. Mucous and blood clots weren't classified as defects unless they were over two centimeters long. And while inspectors had once strived for zero defects, the USDA had set tolerance limits at thirty-five defects per carcass.

"The USDA dropped the most basic principle learned at the dawn of mankind," Mary Heersink, founder of STOP, said during a brief phone conversation with me. "Humans learned early on, probably the hard way, to keep manure off meat. But here, at the end of the second millennium, at the very moment that a new, mutant strain of E. coli appears on the scene, at the very moment that the NAS is screaming for microbial testing and alarms are being sounded by the CDC, the USDA decides that the time has come to establish levels for allowable fecal contamination on meat.

"While epidemiologists measured that one speck of feces can contain millions of microbes of E. coli 0157, and that a mere one to ten microbes can kill a child, USDA bureaucrats were counting how many visible specks and smears of cow feces they would overlook on each animal."

As with poultry, to create an illusion of federal oversight, inspectors were authorized to reinspect six sides of beef—the equivalent of three cows—out of as many as 3,200 cattle per shift. Still, while only three-tenths of 1 percent of the meat leaving the plant was thoroughly examined by government inspectors, 100 percent of it was rubber-stamped "U.S. Inspected and Passed."

"The inspections we perform are toothless," inspectors wrote in a letter to then Secretary of Agriculture Clayton Yeutter. "Under Streamlined Inspection, we are restricted from completing comprehensive inspections, so it is impossible to be sure that contaminated, unwholesome product has not left the plant. We're not allowed to have a good view of the carcasses, and even if we did, the line is going too fast to see well. If we stop the line to condemn contaminated meat or ensure that it is trimmed, we face reprisals from our supervisors. Instead of providing us support, our supervisors impose sanctions on us when we do our jobs."

GAP's Tom Devine verified this for me. "Inspectors who have attempted to stop the line have been reprimanded, reassigned, physically attacked by plant employees and then disciplined for being in fights, had their performance appraisals lowered, been placed under criminal investigation, fired, or been subjected to other forms of retaliation that were necessary to 'neutralize' them."

※　※　※

"A rat came out of the box room and ran across the floor," reads one inspector's affidavit.

The inspector shut down the line after the rat ran across her foot. At that point all the boxes should have been inspected for any more rats as well as for droppings that aren't supposed to be mixed in with the beef. But the veterinarian just laughed, had the floor hosed down, and allowed the line to be turned back on in five to ten minutes. After that, hunting and killing rats turned into something between sport and a bad joke for the inspectors. Company employees told us that rats were all over the coolers at night, running on top of meat and gnawing at it.

It was especially significant that we lost control of contamination. The veterinarians told us, "You're not shit inspectors anymore, you're pathology inspectors only." That would have been pleasant if someone had filled the vacuum when we stopped controlling filth. No one did. As a result, we saw fecal contamination get through—up to one-foot smears—as well as flukes [liver parasites], grubs [wormlike fly larvae that burrow into the cow's skin and work their way through the animal's body], abscesses [encapsulated infections filled with pus], [hide] hair, and ingesta [partially digested food found in the stomach or esophagus].

That account and those that follow, compiled by GAP attorneys, describe the type of beef that was suddenly passing federal inspection. The affidavits came from meat inspectors in all five pilot plants, the very individuals responsible for making Streamlined Inspection work.

"Company managers ordered employees to cut open abscesses and let them drain on healthy portions of meat, instead of trimming off infected areas. Even then, plant employees report incidents such as buying a precooked roast and cutting into a healthy abscess. Manure, hair, hide, metal, and chewing tobacco regularly contaminate products that used to be clean. Cactus thorns stay in beef tongues, because the lines are going too fast for workers to remove them. Cows are slaughtered that have been dead on arrival, some so long they are ice-cold. When plant employees think we aren't looking, they order USDA retain tags* pulled, and ship out carcasses without trimming off open pus-filled abscesses. Inedible meat products full of disease are mixed with edible products. One firm shipped out meat so old it was green when trimmed."

When a Nebraska inspector smuggled head meat out of a plant to run an unauthorized check, he found that "24 percent of the heads reaching the head-boning table for boxing were contaminated with hair, dirt, hide, and ingesta," he said. "The type of heads getting through, including those known in the industry as 'pukeheads,' are so filled with partially digested food that contamination oozes into the outer surfaces of the head and cross-contaminates others." Head meat usually winds up in burgers.

"Every day, carcasses fall on the floor and are not trimmed before the company puts them back on the line. Floors are filthy, covered with blood, grease, feces, pus from abscesses, and mud. A lot gets embedded into the meat from the high-pressure carcass sprays. . . ."

According to another inspector, "Insects have had a feast. Rodent infestation and cockroaches up to two inches long have been prevalent. There are pools of urine on the viscera table that regularly contacts products. The company sprinkled

---

*When an abnormal organ or carcass is detected by an inspector, it is retained for further examination by a USDA veterinarian.

the floor with anti-maggot solution, but the drains are so often stopped up, filthy water splashes on the carcasses even if they don't fall off the rail. . . ."

Yet another offered this observation: "One example of Streamlined 'wholesome' is 'water bellies.' That means urine has backed up and swelled the cow's tissues. This happens when cows can't urinate, because they're clogged up with a condition similar to gallstones. Buckets of urine saturate their briskets, shank, and bellies. It just floods out when the cow is slaughtered. Before Streamlined, any cow like that would have been condemned. Since Streamlined, vets have been approving urine-soaked meat for consumers.

"Another example of Streamlined 'wholesome' is approval of cattle with chronic pneumonia and arthritis. Vets are now approving cattle that wheeze loudly before slaughter, with lungs that are filled with fluid, that have scar tissue and abscesses running all up and down the sides of the lungs and stuck to their ribs, and have popped blood vessels in kidneys that are no longer functional. . . ."

🐝   🐝   🐝

Despite the experts' damning reports, neither scientists, consumer advocates, nor the meat inspectors' union had the clout to get the Streamlined Inspection pilot withdrawn. Congress only showed concern after the pilot program was exposed on network TV. When confronted on ABC's "PrimeTime Live" with videotaped evidence and meat samples documenting feces in our meat supply, the USDA's chief of meat inspection was seen squirming and fumbling for words as he attempted to defend the program. "You're telling me the meat is safe," said the ABC correspondent. "How much fecal matter is allowable in our meat?"

"I'm not sure," replied the USDA official. "I don't have the answer to that. I'll have to ask our experts."

❁   ❁   ❁

As a last-ditch effort at damage control, the USDA convened a panel of industry experts and took them on a tour of the pilot plants. USDA meat inspector David Carney tagged along with the review team and explained in an affidavit what he saw:

> I want to make a record of the bureaucratic games I witnessed as a union observer in the USDA's recent management review. What I saw was a lavish, no-holds-barred hard sell of Streamlined Inspection deregulation by agency management to the consultants on the review team. The USDA turned the review into a big-budget advertising blitz instead of a serious effort to make informed policy choices. They acted like used-car salesmen for Streamlined Inspection.
>
> At the pilot plants we visited, more carcasses were contaminated with more filth than at plants under normal federal inspection coverage. For example, there was more hair, ingesta, fecal stains, and pieces of bone. There were more bruises, some up to the size of a basketball. Streamlined "wholesome" also included many more pizzles—cattle penises —attached to the inner sides of meat that goes into steaks.
>
> None of this increased contamination seemed to bother USDA managers hosting the review. It was the same way with diseases that can harm consumers. For example, due to sloppy corporate practices that camouflage the symptoms, under

Streamlined Inspection hardly any carcasses with "measles" get condemned any more. This bothers me a lot, because cattle "measles" is another name for tapeworms. When this point came up during the review, USDA host Dr. Robert Ragland— one of the leaders in the agency's Streamlined program—said that isn't a significant public health threat, because measles only lead to tapeworms in humans that can be treated. That was an irresponsible position for a public health official. I for one cannot stomach the idea of USDA-approved worms.

Only after further media exposés and considerable pressure from the Government Accountability Project and its federal whistleblowers was the USDA forced to withdraw its request for congressional funding and phase Streamlined Cattle Inspection out.* Streamlined Poultry Inspection was never canceled, and remains in effect to this day.

And, only when I'd seen the mockery meat inspection officials had made of their primary mandate—ensuring meat and poultry wholesomeness—did I really understand just how low a priority humane slaughter was, and why its enforcement was in such shambles.

---

*While termination of Streamlined Cattle Inspection resulted in inspectors being restored to the line, nothing in the phase-out required plants to return to their former line speeds. On the contrary, since the pilot plants had invested thousands of dollars modifying their production lines, and because there were now more inspectors on the line, some plants actually *increased* their slaughter rates. Just by implementing the Streamlined pilot—whether it was successful or not—USDA appointees had managed to institutionalize meteoric line speeds, not only in the pilot plants, but also in nonpilot plants attempting to remain competitive.

15

This Little Piggy Dragged to Market

The man who stepped into my office couldn't possibly be a meat inspector. This man was about six foot four inches tall, in his late forties, wearing a designer suit and expensive cowboy boots. With his silver-gray hair and chiseled good looks he might have been a congressman or a Capitol Hill lobbyist, not someone who spent his days standing in blood and animal guts.

But Dave Carney led a double life. When not inspecting meat for the USDA in an Ohio plant, he could be found courting the media, hobnobbing with senators, and above all representing a bargaining unit of six thousand food inspectors. Carney had worked for nearly two decades as an inspector in both red meat and poultry plants, and was now chairman of the National Joint Council of Food Inspection Locals, the federal meat inspectors' union.

Aware that Carney had been an outspoken opponent of Streamlined Inspection, I set up a meeting to discuss violations of the Humane Slaughter Act. Would I learn that inspectors were lazy, apathetic enforcers of what they viewed as an inconsequential law? Or, would he confirm my growing suspicion that their supervisors had again flexed their bureaucratic muscles to intentionally prevent enforcement of the act?

I found a comfortable chair for him and got us both some coffee. Then I asked him about the USDA's mandate of enforcing humane slaughter regulations.

Carney settled further into the chair and took a sip of coffee.

"How much do you know about what goes on inside packing plants?" he asked.

"Some," I replied.

"Well," he said, "there's a specific problem with enforcing the Humane Slaughter Act. That's because these large slaughtering operations are primarily concerned with productivity and profit." Carney spoke slowly and deliberately. "They don't care about the effects on the animals. It's as if they're not even killing animals. They're 'disassembling' them, processing raw materials in a manufacturing operation.

"To keep that production line moving," he continued, "quite often uncooperative animals are beaten, they have prods poked in their faces and up their rectums, they have bones broken and eyeballs poked out, suspects* are left unattended for days. Sometimes animals are simply beaten to death out in the pens before being slipped into the slaughtering process.

---

*Live animals that appear to be afflicted with a disease or condition that could make them unfit for human consumption.

Some even reach various stages of the slaughtering process alive. They have their hooves cut off, parts of their bung and their cavities opened." For the next several minutes he talked about beating, dragging, prodding, and hit-or-miss stunning.

Finally I was hearing this from someone with clout. "But then, if you know that all these violations go on," I asked, "why don't inspectors do anything about them?"

"First of all," he replied, "the way the plants are physically laid out, meat inspection is way down the line. A lot of times, inspectors can't even see the slaughter area from their stations. It's virtually impossible for them to monitor the slaughter area when they're trying to detect diseases and abnormalities in carcasses that are whizzing by."

I knew that Humane Slaughter Act regulations gave inspectors the authority to stop the line when they saw violations. But I also knew that they did not authorize inspectors to visit the plant's slaughter area hourly, daily, weekly, or ever, for that matter. "So how often does someone go down to the slaughter area and look?" I asked.

"And leave his station?" Carney replied. "If an inspector did that, he'd be subject to disciplinary action for abandoning his inspection duties. Unless he stopped the line first, which would get him into even more trouble. Inspectors are tied to the line."

"So what's the procedure for checking humane slaughter?" I asked.

"There isn't one," he answered.

"Hold on. You're telling me that inspectors have the authority to stop the line when they see humane violations, but basically, they're never allowed to see them?"

"That's right," he said. "Inspectors are required to enforce humane regulations on paper only. Very seldom do they ever go into that area and actually enforce humane handling and slaughter. They can't. They're not allowed to.

"Besides," he continued, "our inspectors are already overwhelmed with their meat inspection duties and the agency has never addressed the responsibility of humane slaughter."

But wait—this didn't let the inspectors off the hook.

"Fair enough," I said. "But I've talked to plenty of workers who say the inspectors see the violations and do nothing about them."

"This comes up all the time on my union job. If you stop a mass-production line, where you have sixty, seventy, a hundred plant employees standing around, your boss, the USDA veterinarian in the plant, is going to make your life hell. He feels he's got to answer to the company for lost production. He'll ridicule you, chew you out. Inspectors are often disciplined for sticking to regulations and stopping production for a *contamination* problem—meat safety—which has a much higher priority than animal suffering. It's a sad state of affairs that we have overburdened inspectors out there who don't get the support of their supervisors."

"But the vets don't have to answer to the industry," I said. "Why don't they just enforce the law?"

Carney drank some more coffee, then smiled. "A lot of the vets think of themselves as in retirement. You even hear them joking about it. They don't do any physical work. As far as veterinary expertise, they're way out of their realm. They're reduced to paperwork. The physical location in the plants where the animals are stuck and bled is a very uninviting work environment. The vets hardly ever go there.

"Let me ask you this," he continued. "Why would someone who'd completed years of higher education to learn how to save animals and make them healthy work for a system that torments and kills animals?"

I asked Carney about the pervasiveness of the types of violations he had described.

"The inspectors I talk to are from all over the country," he replied. "It's an everyday occurrence clear across the United States. It occurs in swine. It occurs in beef. It occurs in calves. Sheep. All species," he explained.

"The Humane Slaughter Act is a regulation on paper only," he reiterated. "It is not being enforced."

※   ※   ※

Dave Carney took me to meet his predecessor at a hotel where the union was holding a conference. Roberto Macias, former chairman of the National Joint Council of Food Inspection Locals, was a bear of a man with dark curly hair and a weathered face. He had worked as a meat inspector for twenty-nine years.

"If you ask agency officials if there's a Humane Slaughter Act," he said, "they'll say yes. But it's not a reality out there. Oh, you might find some isolated pocket where you've got a supervisor who might take the time to ensure compliance. But percentagewise, the answer is no. The Humane Slaughter Act is not being enforced."

Carney nodded.

"Whose fault is that?" I asked Macias.

"It's not right to blame inspectors," he responded. "In a slaughterhouse the supervisory veterinary medical officer is the one who has overall responsibilities. Those meat inspectors, as gently as I can describe it, are just like a bunch of sheep. They're being told what to do. Mostly, they're being told what *not* to do."

"How have these USDA vets led their flock of inspectors so far astray?" I asked.

"Most veterinarians are like the viscosity of oil," Macias said. "They flow along the path of least resistance. Let's say you're the vet. If there's an inspector who's outspoken about these things, you're going to have to confront plant management on a daily basis. You have to decide: Do I side with the inspector, who really doesn't pose any challenge to my authority, or with plant management, who can do me harm because they can go and talk to my circuit supervisor or district manager.* If I'm seen as an oddity in the arena of performance, my rating and my chance for promotion go down, and my chances of getting on the shit list go up. You tell me, which way do you go?"

"We're dictated to by the industry we regulate," Carney added.

All totaled, Macias estimated that as many as 90 percent of vets were not effectively enforcing even meat safety regulations. "And I can't conceive of an inspector stopping the line for humane violations," he said, "because he would be at the mercy of his supervisor. He would be subject to disciplinary action. Because even though the HSA may be in the regulations, there's very little emphasis put on it."

---

*Under the USDA's current organizational structure, slaughterhouse inspectors report to in-plant veterinarians who, in turn, report to one of the country's two hundred circuit supervisors. Circuit supervisors report to eighteen district managers, who are accountable to the USDA's Field Operations in Washington.

"Does any of this have to do with recent increases in line speeds?" I asked.

"You're going to have to excuse my language, Gail," he said. "But in some of those plants it's like trying to stuff ten pounds of crap into a five-pound package. They sure as hell weren't built to take the line speeds they're running at now. So how can USDA management assure the public that meat is safe and animals are being slaughtered humanely? You're asking inspectors to do more with less—less time.

"Take Streamlined Inspection," he continued. "USDA went out and told the industry, 'This is a better system, we're going to do it with fewer inspectors, and we're going to let you perform certain functions that inspectors used to do.' And the incentive they used to get plants to volunteer for the pilot program was that it would allow them to increase their chain speed. And then they say to industry, 'Doggone it, Congress and the American public were made aware that we were not protecting that product the way we should have. So, we're going to take Streamlined Inspection away, but we're going to allow you to maintain your line speeds.'

"See, the USDA approach whenever they try to implement new programs is to say it's an 'improved way' of inspecting," Macias went on. "But it's not the truth. Streamlined wasn't a better inspection system, it was a less-inspector system."

Macias leaned toward me.

"I wish I could dress you up as an inspector and let you work for about a month in IBP* in Kansas. I guarantee you would come back to me with tears in your eyes, and you

---

*IBP is the country's largest beef and pork packer. The plant he referred to is a beef operation.

would hug me and say, 'Now I understand what you're going through when you feel sorry for those inspectors.' "

Macias and Carney also represented thousands of inspectors who work in chicken and turkey plants.

"Poultry is exempt from coverage under the Humane Slaughter Act, right?" I asked.

"Correct," Carney said. "It's not humanely slaughtered. Because they're going into the scald tanks still alive, breathing and sucking in the water."

Macias nodded. "Most of them are still alive when they go into that tank and they fill their lungs. That's a reason for the high contamination."

"The kicker," Carney said, "is that when that chicken is exported to Canada, inspectors have to sign off on an export certificate that says it's been humanely slaughtered. We have no control over how they're slaughtered. None whatsoever."

"What about the export of red meat?" I asked.

"No monitoring of that whatsoever," Carney said.

"So you're saying it's a sham that the USDA says exported meat products are humanely slaughtered?"

"That's a good word for it," Macias said.

"It's fraud," Carney said.

"Then isn't it fraud here in the United States when Americans are eating meat that they think has been slaughtered in compliance with the HSA?"

Macias nodded. "Sure it is," he said.

"It's part of our regulatory responsibility that we never enforce," said Carney.

"And there's quite a few things that we don't enforce," Macias added. "Through no choice of our own.

"It's a you-scratch-my-back-and-I'll-scratch-yours thing,"

Macias continued, "designed to accommodate the industry. If the inspectors charged with enforcing humane regulations don't have any oversight over humane slaughter, who does?

"We're regulatory enforcement officers," Macias continued. "We're given a badge. We're more or less like the Border Patrol. We don't have arrest powers or the authority to carry arms, but we do have an important regulatory function to perform on behalf of the American public."

Macias leaned forward again. "Is that regulatory function limited to what we can see immediately in front of us with tunnel vision?" he asked in disgust. "It certainly shouldn't be, but that's just what the USDA and the industry want."

※   ※   ※

Carney introduced me to some other inspectors, telling them they could talk to me frankly without fear of reprisal.

"You may see a broken leg on postmortem," said an Illinois inspector. "You may see some busted ribs. After a certain length of time working as an inspector, you know that hog was mishandled, but you didn't see it happen so you can't do anything about it. You can't be every place in the plant at once."

"We don't see 95 percent of what's going on," said a female inspector from a small Ohio plant. "For instance, an ex-employee recently told me about a cow who got her leg stuck when the floor of a truck collapsed. 'How'd you get her out alive?' I asked the guy. 'Oh,' he said, 'we just went underneath the truck and cut her leg off.' If somebody tells you this, you know there's a lot of things nobody's telling you."

"The way the plants are set up," said an Indiana inspector, "we aren't in a position to see what's going on. In a lot of plants, the slaughter area is walled off from the rest of the kill floor. Yes, we should be monitoring slaughter. But how can you monitor something like that if you're not allowed to leave your station to see what's going on?"

"Dragging cattle with a chain and a forklift is standard practice at the plant," explained a long-term inspector at a large beef operation in Nebraska. "And that's even after the forklift operator rolled over and crushed the head of one downer while dragging another."

He went on to tell me about a cow who got away from the plant for several days. That Friday afternoon the manager and a few others jumped into a pickup truck and hunted her down. Using a high-powered rifle, they shot her in the gut, and when she tried to run away they pumped several more rounds into her. The bullet that blew off her jawbone also finally brought her down.

"They made a big adventure of it," he said. "They were chasing her down, shooting out of the four-wheel drive. To them it was fun."

"What about the vet?"

"The vet's an old guy who pretty much allows things to happen that never should. And any time an inspector makes a stand, he gets subjected to," he sighed, "our own people. Is he right or wrong? The regulations are kind of vague, subject to interpretation. There's people who'll say it all depends on how you read it. It's easy to ignore things.

"One time there was a problem, I shut the line down. One of their people gets in my face, starts yelling, calling me dirty names. I called the foreman over, told him if it happens again, I'm going to shut the line down and we're going inside to discuss it. It happened again. When it got to my superiors that the company tried to intimidate me, they asked how I knew it was directed at me. I said he's two feet away from me, screaming in my face, using my name. My superior says maybe there's someone else out there with the same name as me."

I asked a veteran USDA inspector who worked at a modern, high-speed plant in Texas if he ever saw violations of the HSA or had difficulty enforcing it.

"Like torching off an animal's leg?" he asked. "A steer was running up the alleyway and got his leg between the boards and he couldn't get it out. They didn't want to lose any time killing cattle, and he was blocking their path, so they just used a blow torch to burn his leg off while he was alive."

"Any other types of violations?" I asked.

"Cattle dragged and choked, stuff like that. Knocking 'em four, five, ten times. Every now and then when they're stunned they come back to life, and they're up there agonizing. They're supposed to be restunned but sometimes they aren't and they'll go through the skinning process alive. I saw that myself, a bunch of times. I've found them alive clear over to the rump stand."*

"How long does it take an animal to get there?" I asked.

"They've been completely legged," he said. "Ten minutes maybe.† And they run them through an electrical shock system, too."

"The stimulator [a device that passes electrical current through the body to improve meat color and texture]?" I asked.

"Yeah."

---

*The plant area where the hide is cut off the hindquarters.

†The bottom parts of the legs have been removed while the top parts have been skinned. At this point, the animal has been transferred from a shackle to having meat hooks inserted into each exposed ankle.

"Maybe they weren't alive," I said. "Could it just be muscle reaction?"

"When they're sucking in air and bellowing, their eyes bugging out? Sometimes they fall through the bottom of that restrainer and they're still alive. And the workers have to get them up anyway they can. So, they wrap a chain around it, lift it up, bust something. If it's a leg, they'll break the leg. If it's the head, they'll break the neck. It usually breaks, whatever they hook on to. You can hear the bones cracking a lot of times.

"And that happens in *every* plant," he said. "I've worked in four large ones and a bunch of small ones. They're all the same. If people were to see this, they'd probably feel really bad about it. But in a packing house everybody gets so used to it that it doesn't mean anything."

"Do you do anything about it?" I asked.

"When I happen to see it," he replied. "There's a lot of people that'll disagree with humane groups about killing cattle. They say, well, they've got to kill them. All the vets will say, 'Those humane people are real crackpots, these are big old beasts and we've got to kill them somehow.' I'm sure you've heard that. But there are quicker ways to handle them."

I asked a group of inspectors who worked on a large Midwest hog kill floor about the veterinarians they worked with.

"Most of the vets are from foreign countries," explained an inspector. "They've never had a job as good as this one, and they don't want to rock the boat."

A woman laughed. "You aren't going to find any vets down in that blood pit."

"They're not interested in the kill," said a man.

"Our vets wear ties and nice shirts," said another.

"After all," said another inspector, "blood shows up on khaki pants."

* * *

Luther Johnson had worked for several years as the only meat inspector at a Midwest distress kill, the end of the line for worn-out, sick, or crippled hogs. "Most of these animals aren't that old," he said, "they're just abused. Malnourished, frostbit, injured. Lot of DOAs [dead on arrivals]. Sows with broken pelvises who pull themselves around with their front legs, scooting along on their rumps for so long they get emaciated. They call them 'scooters.' " The meat from these distress kills, if it passes inspection, is used for sausage, hot dogs, pork by-products, and ham. If the animal is condemned, then it is rendered for use in animal feed, cosmetics, plastics, and a whole host of household and industrial products.

"One day when I went out to the suspect pen, two employees, one from a local rendering company, were using metal pipes to club some hogs to death. There had to be twenty little hogs out there that they were going to give to the rendering company. And these two guys were out there beating them with clubs and having a good old time.

"I went to the vet, my supervisor, to complain. He said, 'They're of no value because they're going to be tanked* anyway.' So, according to my supervisor, it was all right to club those little hogs to death. They were beating them like they do those little seals in Alaska."

"Have you worked only at distress kills?" I asked him.

---

*Rendered.

"I've been in dozens of different plants. Not stationed in all of them," he said, "just on detail for a week or two. I've seen dump trucks dump piles of cripples from eight feet off the ground. I've seen cattle get to leggers fully conscious, get their front legs skinned and hind legs cut off, then go to the flankers where a worker takes the hide off with an air knife.*

"At this plant here, workers drag cripples with a garden tractor and a chain—that's the only way they move cripples here. I asked the owner, 'Why don't you get a Bobcat?' He says, 'This garden tractor's good enough.' Then I brought it to the attention of my supervisor and he thought it was unimportant. 'They've been doing this for twenty years,' he said. 'Why change now? Nobody's been hurt.'"

"Why do you think the vets ignore this?" I asked.

He didn't seem to hear me. I'd seen this with many of the plant workers and USDA employees I'd interviewed—once they start talking about what they'd seen and done, they want to get it all off their chests.

"Just last week a hog got her head stuck in a gate and the workers broke two of her legs pulling her out," he said. "Then, since she couldn't walk through the chute to be stunned, they wrapped a cable around her snout and dragged her up alive. You know what that cable does to the snout when you're dragging a hog that weighs several hundred pounds? The company defended the workers and blamed the poor hog, saying, 'She didn't want to go.'

"I've seen them put twenty to twenty-five holes in a hog's head trying to knock her and she was still on her feet. Her head looked like Swiss cheese. Tough gal. Sometimes the captive

_____

*An air-powered (pneumatic) circular blade that whirls around.

bolt won't work at all so they'll use a twenty-two and shoot the hog through its eye. Or you might have to hit both eyes on the same hog."

"What happens when you try to do something about violations?" I asked.

"I had one guy threaten me with a pistol because I was watching him hang suspects and I stopped operations. But these problems are pretty much across the board. At some plants you have authority, at others you don't. It all comes down to the veterinarian, who doesn't want you to undermine him or her, buck their authority, do a better job than them. 'I'm the boss here, I'll find the problems. You go back on the line.' The regulations don't require them to go down to the stick pit, they probably don't go down there once a month.

"You talk to any inspector who's been around any length of time. Vets and supervisors do the minimal amount of work required of them, mostly making everything look good on paper. As for making sure plants are in compliance with regs, they're very lax. Most of them get into government work because they're too lazy to have their own practices. They'd have to work, they might have to go out to the barn in the middle of the night and pull [deliver] a calf. Here they can work a seven to three-thirty job, sit in their office, read the newspaper and do crossword puzzles, and drink a lot of coffee. . . .

"Actually, there have been times, I admit, when I've been outside and could see something was going to happen. I knew I wouldn't get the support from my supervisor so I'd walk back inside because I didn't want to see it. Not that I turned my back on it. I just couldn't do anything about it. I didn't want to see a hog's leg jerked off or something. The veterinarians are the ones screwing up, and the inspectors are being blamed."

16

Veterinary Turncoats

"An animal that was shackled on the line past the first hock cutter was bellowing," wrote a USDA veterinarian in an internal memo to her circuit supervisor.

"The chain was stopped while this animal was re-stunned. This animal, because it was not stunned properly or stuck properly so that it bled enough to lose consciousness, experienced the following: (1) electric shocks from the stimulator; (2) its hide being cut open first from the belly to the rectum, then from the cuts to clear the hock of hide for cutting*; (3) both forelegs being cut off with cutters; (4) its hock being cut off and then the end of its tail being cut off with cutters; (5) the

---

*"Cuts" here means "midline incision"—all the cuts branch off the original cut down the belly—to the knee joint.

rest of its hide being removed from its right hind leg by air knives.

"I have timed the path this animal had traveled from stun chute to being rendered insensible at about $9\frac{1}{2}$ minutes."

This internal memo, which represents one of the rare instances in which a USDA veterinarian reported a violation of the Humane Slaughter Act, was leaked to me through an inside source at the USDA.

＊　＊　＊

"Veterinarians are caught in the middle," GAP's Tom Devine said. "Often an inspector may think a veterinarian is responsible for an illegal or obnoxious policy because the vet announced it. Same thing with nonenforcement of a regulation—it looks like it's the vet's idea when in reality the vets are little better than messengers from headquarters to inspectors on the front line. They get overruled. In some cases, vets have ended up taking the heat and becoming whistleblowers to support concerns that inspectors had reported to them."

According to Devine, in-plant veterinarians and their immediate superiors—circuit supervisors—often have similar viewpoints on how the law should be enforced. It's their bosses in Washington who almost always place agribusiness interests above consumer safety and animal welfare.

"The meat industry's high-powered lobbying usually starts at the district level and extends through headquarters," Devine said. "Those officials, by and large, are bureaucrats or paper-pushers who develop the regulatory policy. From the circuit level on down, the staff work in meat plants. They're the ones who get their hands dirty."

*   *   *

I made an appointment to meet with Dr. Lester Friedlander, a USDA veterinarian who patrolled several slaughter plants in Pennsylvania. That weekend I drove to eastern Pennsylvania, where he and his family were attending a high school wrestling championship. After the first day's matches, Friedlander, an engaging, scrappy, Joe Pesci sound-alike about five feet five inches tall, invited me to his motel room to talk. He'd been with the agency for nine years, receiving many accolades for excellence, and was once awarded Trainer of the Year for his instruction in pathology to new veterinarians.

"I don't think too many USDA veterinarians are going to talk to you," he said. "They don't want to get in my situation, getting harassed by the agency." Friedlander, an outspoken critic of the USDA, alleges retaliation by Washington supervisors in response to his vocal complaints about agency practices. "At this point in my career it doesn't bother me one bit," he said, "because I know the USDA is wrong. I see how they work, how they've deceived and lied."

He'd talked about bad meat and human health hazards. I asked about enforcement of the Humane Slaughter Act.

"USDA veterinarians do have the freedom to walk around the plant," he explained, "but they don't concentrate on HSA violations. Their main job is pathology. The inspector's job is only to retain something—that means putting a tag on it so the veterinarian will examine it. When the veterinarian gets it, he does an investigation to learn the extent of the condition—whether it's localized or generalized—by looking at the animal's lymph nodes and organs. He puts everything together like a puzzle to determine what disease condition the animal has, then he goes to the carcass and makes the final disposition. So he's busy dealing with that."

"Do the vets—or the inspectors, for that matter—ever look for HSA violations?" I asked.

"If the veterinarian has enough time, he should be walking through the kill floor to look at things, going into the pen area to see if there are any downers, to see what's going on. He should be supervising. But you can't supervise when you've got to work the line.

"In most plants, inspectors are only required to look at 5 to 10 percent of [live] animals in motion, so most of the time no one's seeing what goes on in the pens. On the other hand, the inspectors on large kill floors are usually a few hundred feet from the stunning area, and there's so much equipment between them that they can hardly see what's going on over there.

"Let's say you have seven inspectors on the line," he continued. "The line is moving and each inspector's station has a specific job. Now, say one of the inspectors who's supposed to be examining the hearts tells the plant foreman to call you— the vet—and tell you something inhumane is going on. As a supervisor, the first thing you're going to ask is, 'How do you know that was happening? If you saw that, then who was doing your job?' That's neglect of duty.

"Compounding the problem is that a lot of plants don't have roving inspectors. The ones that do are usually so short-staffed that the roving inspectors have to work the line."

"What *should* happen?" I asked.

"At every inspection station on the kill floor there's a stop button," Friedlander explained. "If an inspector sees anything wrong, he has the authority to hit that stop button. He's the only one who can give the company permission to turn it on again. If there's a gap in the line, some downtime—or a machine breaks, and he looks around and sees an animal that isn't stunned properly or is running around with its neck cut open—he has the right to stop everything and make sure the condition is corrected.

"But," he continued, "veterinarians and inspectors sometimes look the other way. In a small town, like where I live, the plant is the biggest employer around. USDA and plant employees and supervisors go to the movies together, they bowl together, socialize in various ways. If you try to get something done in the plant as an inspector and you're friends with the plant supervisor, and the supervisor says, 'Why don't you cut me a break and just go easy?' what are you going to do? That's the kind of stuff that happens all the time. Instead of making the right decisions, inspectors are looking the other way.

"And there's nobody there to regulate it. You make the decisions. How often does your circuit supervisor come around? He's supposed to come around once a month to check on you. But, because the circuits are so big, unless there's a problem, he mostly visits plants closest to home. In some of these places, circuit supervisors don't even come around once every two or three months.

"Meanwhile the company tries to turn everything to its advantage. The fewer people they need to get the job done, the better off they are, because the bottom line in this industry is the cost-effectiveness. A lot of these packers experiment on their own without letting USDA know about it. There's always a game of cat and mouse with the packers. Happens all the time. And we're always at a disadvantage, because the plant tries to pull something, and we have to figure out what was wrong.

"Blood clots cause extra work," he explained, "because

they are classified as a defect and have to be removed. If the plant now needs more workers to remove blood clots, management is going to say, 'How can we change that? Well, let's experiment. We'll change some things around and we won't tell the USDA. We'll change the air pressure. We won't use the bigger captive bolt. We'll use a small one and see what happens. And if that works we're going to keep it that way no matter if the regulations call for humane slaughter.'

"Another example is when workers are told to cut contamination away. A lot of plant workers will take their knife and gouge half a pound of meat off. And then the company will look at this and say, 'Gosh, half a pound times fifteen hundred head, that's a lot of meat we lost.' So every chance they get, when there isn't an inspector looking, they'll take a conveniently placed hose and just wash it off. When you stick a hose to contamination, all you're doing is spreading it.

"Also, plants clean up when they know the USDA is coming down," Friedlander continued. "It's a guessing game because a lot of plants work with hand-held radios. So when they see someone going down to a certain section, all they do is get on the radio and say, 'Hey Joe, the veterinarian's coming your way because I see him walking through the coolers.' The packers have an overwhelming advantage over us. We're just playing the catch-up game."

"I've heard vets don't go down to the blood pit very often," I said.

"There are probably some who only go down there once a month. Some don't want to get involved. They don't want to make a big stink that ends up coming back to them. They'd rather have an inspector bring a violation to their attention so they can blame it on the inspector and keep their distance from the problem. And it makes them look a little bit better. That way, when it gets to their circuit supervisor and he makes a big deal out of it, the vet can say to him, 'Well, this inspector is the one who told me this.' And it's the same thing with the plant. When a plant manager challenges the USDA veterinarian, the vet says, 'It was the inspector that mentioned it. I didn't see it.'

"Nobody wants to handle it because nobody wants to stick their neck out. And then, if you talk to a veterinarian who is foreign-born—which many of them are—right away he gets intimidated by a plant official, an American who says, 'Hey, you're working in my country, this is my business, don't tell me how to operate it or I'll call up your bosses and you won't have a job.' Foreign veterinarians are always afraid their jobs are on the line.

"But it's not just the fault of the USDA veterinarians in the plants. We don't get the support of our supervisors in the circuits, districts, and in Washington. We get our orders from the circuit supervisor. They don't want to get involved, get their careers all screwed up, so they leave you there to hang. They say, 'Well, if you can't handle this and you've got so many complaints about the plant, then I suggest you go take another job. Or, if you want me to, I'll find somebody to replace you.'

"Likewise, when the USDA issued regulations in 1979 to assure the consumer that animals were being humanely handled and slaughtered, it was only paperwork. Really. It's only a big cover-up. Because when we try to enforce the regulations at the lowest level, our supervisors in Washington start hiding. They don't want to hear anything about it."

"All that's the stick," I said. "By any chance is there a carrot?"

Friedlander laughed. "Some of the vets want to cover

themselves or go easy on the plants because they know that after they leave the USDA they can get a high-paying job as an industry consultant. Our supervisors, too. They're supposed to be the people who regulate the industry, and every time we pass a decision up to them from the field, they shoot it back down at us, telling us to work it out. They're just trying to cover themselves for the future so when they retire they can get a job as a consultant.

"Like with a good friend of mine, a USDA veterinarian up at a Minnesota plant for twenty-five years. When he retired, before the paperwork was finalized, the slaughterhouse sent out a letter saying that he was now the plant's veterinarian."*

"A vet I knew out in Dallas worked for the USDA thirty-some years, regional director the last five. Shortly after he retired, he became a consultant for some of the largest plants over which he'd had jurisdiction. Now he's financially set, he's getting a consulting fee on top of his USDA pension."

Friedlander then named fourteen former USDA executives he personally knew who had recently moved directly into industry jobs. "Not just vets," he explained. "Training officers,

---

*There are two federal laws that prohibit former government employees from representing the regulated industry before their former agencies. The first, the "post-employment statute" (18USC §207), bans federal employees from advocating on behalf of the reg- ulated industry for a period of two years. The second, Executive Order 12834 of 1993, imposes similar restrictions on high-ranking federal appointees for a period of five years. According to the fed- eral ethics handbook, these laws, intended to "prevent employees from 'switching sides,' " carry heavy criminal penalties. When it comes to the USDA, however, these post-employment statutes go completely unenforced.

area supervisors, regional directors, agency administrators, Washington staff officers."

It was past midnight. Dr. Friedlander's children were asleep in the next room. I didn't have any more specific questions for him, but neither of us was satisfied that he'd said everything he had to say. He agreed to finish our talk first thing in the morning.

At 5:30 A.M. he knocked on my door, bearing two containers of coffee. We each took a sip, then I turned the tape recorder back on.

"There's another thing that really bothers me," he said. "In the summertime, when it's ninety, ninety-five degrees, they're transporting cattle from twelve to fifteen hundred miles away on a trailer, forty to forty-five head crammed in there, and some collapse from heat exhaustion. This past winter we had minus-fifty-degree weather with the windchill. Can you imagine if you were in the back of a trailer that's open and the windchill factor is minus fifty degrees, and that trailer is going fifty to sixty miles an hour? The animals are urinating and defecating right in the trailers, and after a while, it's going to freeze, and their hooves are right in it. If they go down—well, you can imagine lying in there for ten hours on a trip. But USDA doesn't step in and say, 'Hey, hold it. The weather's too cold, you can't transport those animals.'

"And when hogs are left lying around the parking lot in a moribund state, dying—USDA doesn't really want to do anything about it. Nobody wants to get involved because the packers are so powerful. You know, the wheels of justice may turn slowly, but the wheels of the United States Department of Agriculture don't turn at all."

He seemed to have run out of steam. I thanked him for taking the time, and the risk, to speak to me.

"There are a lot of things going on that USDA employees don't want to talk about," he said. "They see it, but they don't want to say anything about it. People who've been working for USDA longer than I have say, 'Just don't say anything about it, because you can be retaliated against.' It's taboo. You're in a fraternity where you keep things to yourself.

"A USDA compliance officer once said to me: 'What you're really doing is not protecting the consumer, you're protecting the agency.' Think about that. The agency is at fault, and we're covering up for them."

17

The Thumper

Armed with my new evidence, I decided to give "60 Minutes" another shot. I felt confident that with several USDA meat inspectors and at least one USDA veterinarian willing to go on national television about the agency's nonenforcement of federal law, Mike Wallace and his producer would jump at the chance.

"I don't have time to get into this again right now," the producer said.

"But you and Mr. Wallace thought it was a good story," I pleaded. "Now I've got this great videotaped interview with the chairman of the meat inspectors' union who lays the whole thing out. At least look at the tape."

The producer reminded me that the show's executive producer had considered the story line "too disgusting" from the start, and that he'd already gone against his boss's wishes when he'd met me in Sioux Falls. Now, despite my desperate pleas, he didn't feel that he could pursue a story that his boss didn't support.

"Sorry," he said.

※   ※   ※

I met with the late former U.S. senator and presidential candidate Paul Tsongas, who had previously lobbied Congress on a variety of animal protection issues. While he'd been deeply moved by my documentation, and offered potential legislative angles, he, too, felt strongly that the only way to ensure congressional action—and prompt meaningful change for the animals—would be to nationally televise the exposé.

I sent the videotape to the "20/20" producer, who said he'd pitch the story once again. The senior producer loved it, but the show's executive producer was unmoved. His apparent reasoning was that the subject matter was too graphic for the viewing public.

I pitched the story to two more news shows and got the same response.

One night, with a ball of rage knotted up in my chest, I sat in front of the TV. First I watched the nightly news—a solid half hour of war, starvation, and genocide. Then, channel surfing, I saw several shootings; one rape; a graphic made-for-TV movie about incest; a show in which the hero, a cop, beats a confession out of a prisoner; and a hospital drama with blood and guts galore. All on network TV, all early to late evening.

This was what they broadcast to people who were too fragile to hear the truth about the food they fed their families?

＊　＊　＊

Not knowing where to turn to get the story told, I continued documenting violations, convinced that if I had enough evidence, we could somehow force Congress's hand. I randomly selected a plant on which I'd received no leads. It was a high-speed Monfort operation in Nebraska that ran at about three hundred fifty cattle an hour. Since I had received no complaints about this plant, I didn't know what I would find.

Without informants—as when I first went to Morrell's Sioux Falls plant—my most successful line of approach had been through the union. Monfort's fledgling union was able to put me in touch with a former knocker, Miguel Fernandez, a soft-spoken family man who lived in a small house filled with children and parakeets.

"There's always been problems with the knockers," he started. "There's not enough power to stun the beef, so you have to hit every one, like, eight times."

"You ever complain?" I asked.

"I *always* complained," he replied. "To the foremen. But the maintenance guys always blamed the knocker."

"Is this still going on?" I asked.

"I have a friend who's a legger there," Fernandez said. "He gets beef that's still conscious all the time. Sometimes almost every one. They're looking around, mooing, trying to look up when they're hanging," he said. "After they're knocked, they get up and stumble around like they're drunk."

"How do they handle cripples?" I asked.

"They put a big long chain around her neck then drag her all the way up to where we are. Usually she's dead by then, strangled."

"That's against the law," I said.

"Yeah," he agreed, "the USDA inspectors don't like that. They put a tag on the cable saying not to use it. The foremen would take the tag off and tell us to use it anyway, when the USDA wasn't around. And beef that have died outside, the foreman will put it on the line before the USDA finds out. Sometimes pulled off a truck, sometimes overnighters, sometimes stiff. That's real illegal, too. The cow could've been sick and died. Who knows?

"Sometimes a steer would get its head stuck in the restrainer," he continued. "You couldn't stun it at that point, so you'd end up cutting its head off while the beef was still alive. Or, there have been a lot of cases where the beef almost falls through the restrainer, and it struggles and twists so bad that the restrainer wouldn't move. A lot of times what happens is we just chop the leg off."

"How?" I asked.

"With a saw."

"Before it's knocked?"

He nodded.

"How long do they have to bleed out?"

"Nothing."

"It takes a few minutes for a stuck cow to bleed out," I said. "That's what I mean, how long do they have?"

"That's what I mean—*nothing*. From the sticker to the legger is maybe ten seconds. They're breathing real hard over there, mooing, they're falling off the rail because they're alive.

"And there's only one guy to stick all three thousand beef we do all day," he continued. "So, if he gets behind, he doesn't care. He'll catch up later. He just sticks them wherever he can.

Sometimes he sticks them while the legger's doing his job. Sometimes he sticks them *after* the legger."

"No."

"They *do*. And you can tell it hasn't been stuck, because you can see all the blood coming out during legging and skinning. I've also seen him stick at the hook trolley,"* Fernandez said, "the second hock cutter, left butt, even close to the ears and horns. You can feel all the blood splashing all over at those stations because the beef hasn't been bled.

"I've seen beef still alive at the flankers, more often at the 'ears and horns.' That's a long way. I've seen them over where they take the hide off with the down puller.† I've heard them moo when people with air knives were trying to take the hide off. I think it's cruel for the animal to be dying little by little while everybody's doing their various jobs on it."

"Would the USDA see them alive?"

"Alive and twisting, trying to look up. He'd tell the foreman but not the guys who work there."

"Would they shut the line down?"

"And lose all that money?" he asked. "Time is money in that place."

"But it's not the USDA's money," I said.

Fernandez shrugged. "I've seen a lot of times the USDA should have stopped the line. And they never do."

❋ ❋ ❋

---

*This is where the cow is switched from hanging by a shackle to having meat hooks inserted into each ankle joint.

†A machine that literally peels the hide from the animal's carcass.

While in the Midwest I had to check out a few other leads I'd gotten. My investigation so far had focused on slaughterhouses, but cruelty to farm animals—and the conditions that lead to the proliferation of pathogens and meat contamination—start the day and place the animals are born. There'd been a lot of news coverage lately about the devastating environmental impacts of huge mega-hog farms, the odors, and the deadly microbe pfiesteria that is killing fish and causing open sores and memory loss in fishermen as massive quantities of hog manure seep into waterways.

I already knew that on factory farms that produce millions of hogs each year, breeding hogs, especially the females or sows, spend their entire lives inside tiny metal cages so small that they can never walk or even turn around. The practice, called "crating," has been outlawed on the grounds of cruelty in several European nations. Provided no bedding so dung can fall through to the waste pit below, sows are forced to live— eat, sleep, defecate, give birth, and nurse their young—on concrete or metal-slatted flooring. They inhale the noxious fumes of their own waste, and develop severe respiratory disorders.

I'd made arrangements to interview some former and current hog factory workers. The first one told me that employees had to wear respirators just to do their jobs or they would gag or vomit from the dust and fumes. Another, a woman in her thirties, said that sows, after living on concrete for years, can develop such painful leg conditions that many collapse. Unable to reach their feed, they die of starvation.

"On the farm where I work," she said, "they drag the live ones who can't stand up any more out of the crate. They put a metal snare around her ear or foot and drag her the full length of the building. These animals are just screaming in pain.

They're dragging them across the concrete, it's ripping their skin, the metal snares are tearing up their ears." Worn-out sows are then dumped on a pile, where they stay—for up to two weeks—until the cull truck picks them up.*

"The slaughtering part doesn't bother me," the worker said. "It's the way they're treated when they're alive."

Because germs luxuriate in the filthy, crowded quarters and spread freely from animal to animal, workers are required to shower in and out of the barn and are provided protective clothing by the company, right down to their underwear. Despite those precautions, the very same untrained workers, not veterinarians, administer drugs to sick animals, often by injection. According to one worker who administers medication, what drugs and dosages they use are a matter of "trial and error."

"I'd use the same needle on a hundred pigs, till you couldn't poke it in the skin anymore. Or till it broke. Then I'd have to get a pair of pliers and pull the needle out." The residue of these drugs can wind up in bacon next to the consumer's morning eggs.

Then I was told about the beatings. When the pregnant pigs are ready to give birth, they are moved into different crates. "They beat the shit out of them to get them inside the crates because they don't want to go. This is their only chance to walk around, get a little exercise, and they don't want to go," a worker said. Another employee at a different farm described the routine use of gate rods to beat the sows bloody. "One guy smashed a sow's nose in so bad that she ended up dying of starvation."

---

*Cull trucks pick up worn out, disabled, or dying animals for delivery to distress plants and renderers.

Since uniform size is so important to packers, piglets that don't grow quite fast enough—the "runts"—are quickly weeded out. Picked up by their hind legs, thousands are swung and then bashed headfirst onto the concrete floor. This standard practice used by mega-farm workers is called "thumping."

"We've thumped as many as 120 in one day," said a worker from a Missouri farm. "We just swing them, thump them, then toss them aside. Then, after you've thumped ten, twelve, fourteen of them, you take them to the chute room and stack them up for the dead truck. And if you go in the chute room and some are still alive," he continued, "then you have to thump them all over again. There've been times I've walked in that room and they'd be running around with an eyeball hanging down the side of their face, just bleeding like crazy, or their jaw would be broken."

"We had a total of 138 one day," said a female worker from a different farm. "These animals have the courage to make it through the first thumping, and then *I* have to go and thump them again."

"They call it euthanasia," said the Missouri worker's wife. "The slickest I've ever seen anybody thump a pig was the company vet."

"Some of the guys thump them then just stand on their throats," said the husband, "and wait till they die. I mean, they break their jaws and everything else while they're doing it."

"I've raised horses," said another worker from a different farm, "I've raised pigs. Sure I get frustrated with them sometimes, but I don't sit there and beat them half to death. They're just like children. We got two kids, you can't go at them."

"We spank them," said his wife, who also worked at the facility. "But we don't spank them to death."

18

The Guardian Angel

While in the Midwest, I telephoned Steve Parrish's mother to determine his whereabouts. Now out of jail, he was working in a slaughterhouse near South Bend, Indiana.

He invited me down to hear about it. I arrived in South Bend that evening, called Steve from my motel, and made a date to pick him up in half an hour.

Steve lived in an old house in a dilapidated neighborhood. He greeted me at his door with a warm smile and a long, gentle handshake, then introduced me to his girlfriend—it wasn't BethAnn. A child started crying, and the woman headed upstairs. Steve glanced at her, then back at me and lifted an eyebrow.

"I know a nice little bar where we can kick back, relax," he said, "on the other side of town."

"Let's go."

The parking lot outside the bar was full of cars, motorcycles, and litter. The door opened and two men staggered out in a gust of raunchy music.

As we walked in, I saw a woman on a small stage twirl her bikini top in time to the music and then drop it to the floor. In the course of my job, I'd insinuated myself into many unusual circumstances, but this was not going to be one of them.

"It's too noisy in here to talk," I said. "Let's get out of here."

We drove around until I spotted another bar, this one with an Irish name and a green neon shamrock in the window. I bought us each a beer.

"So what've you been up to?" I asked.

"Staying out of trouble," he said. "So far, anyway."

"And the new job?"

More animals, more abuse.

"And how *you* doing?" he asked.

I told him about the investigation, the media, how frustrating it was to document something so fully and not be able to do anything with it. When I finished, he looked me directly in the eye.

"I know what you going through, Gail," he said quietly. "And I'm going to help." He touched the back of my hand with his index finger. "I'm going to be your guardian angel."

I couldn't have chosen a more unlikely candidate to be my guardian angel. A horse-torturing ex-con with drug convictions. And yet, I was deeply touched by his choice of words.

"Oh right," I said. "Like you can get me and my video camera into your plant?"

"Better'n that," he replied. "I'll video it for you."

"You could do that?" I asked.

He patted my hand. "Just leave it to me."

We went to pick up the camera from my motel room, and soon I was driving him home.

I left my camcorder in South Bend with Steve and drove to Ohio to meet an informant who'd told me the stunning equipment at his plant was faulty and he'd often see live cows hanging from the rail.

I toured the plant with a worker who, at my request, asked the foreman if I could shoot photographs. I shot several rolls of film of the knocker pounding away at each cow's head at least five times.

There was something about being in this plant that was different—it was the closest I'd ever come while undercover to feeling sad about what I saw. There in the stick pit, shooting photos of twenty massive dairy cows hanging before me, I felt tears well up in my eyes for a split second, and then just as quickly disappear. It must have been the size of those mighty beasts that struck me as they dangled from the overhead rail. As they traveled along the chain toward the worker who would cut out their udders, I looked up at them and could still feel their powerful presences lingering from moments before. Yet, as they passed through the blood pit, I was surrounded by their empty shells. The feeling of sadness washed over me and soon I found myself standing up by the stun operator, back to feeling nothing and getting splashed with brains.

When I got back to Washington, D.C., I tried to call Steve Parrish about his plans to help me. No answer, and no answer the dozen more times I called over the next couple of weeks. The last call I made got me a recorded message that the number was no longer in service. Damn. I'd *trusted* this guy. For all I knew, he might have sold the camera to buy drugs.

A week later BethAnn, the woman who'd visited Steve in prison, called me. Shortly after I last saw him, Steve became just another statistic to the Chicago Police Department. My "guardian angel" was stabbed over fifty times and stuffed into his mother's garbage can to die.

19

The Secretary of Agriculture Erects a Smokescreen

I was walking through a gray and bloody hog kill. A foreman grabbed me by the arm and threw me to the concrete floor, wrapped a metal shackle around my ankle, and hoisted me high up on the chain. Hogs were dangling on both sides of me, the conveyor was pulling me toward the sticker who would slit my throat.

"Help me!" I shouted at the top of my lungs. "I am not a hog!" But the clanking of shackles, the din of the chain, the shrill squeal of hogs drowned me out. No one could hear me.

Just as I arrived at the sticker to have my throat cut, I jolted awake from my deep sleep—sweating, out of breath, my heart pounding in my chest.

☀   ☀   ☀

"Patient continues to have a lot of symptoms both GI and recently some problem with regard to breathing," read my doctor's report. "She states that at night sometimes she is afraid that she is going to stop breathing. Recently this has caused her to wake every few minutes throughout the night, and she hasn't been able to get any rest. She talks a lot about the stresses of her job, where she has been privilege to a lot of dreadful things that are happening to animals. She mentions the fact that another investigator who worked with her has had similar problems and has recently handed in her resignation."

※   ※   ※

"There's no history of breast cancer in my family," I said to a co-worker, "but I'm so stressed out, it will be amazing if I don't get it." I'd never had a serious illness in my life, but I knew that a theoretical link had been established between high stress and cancer, and I felt both my body and my spirit giving out.

※   ※   ※

By this time, Timothy Walker had been jobless for over a year. With the help of Government Accountability Project lawyers, I prepared his whistleblower appeal summarizing the violations he'd observed while working at Kaplan Industries in Florida. All totaled, I listed violations of fourteen humane and safety regulations ranging from improper stunning of cattle and the skinning of their heads while still alive, to the fact that shackles and cattle often fell from the rail, posing a serious threat to workers below.

Under the federal Whistleblower Protection Act, once Walker's allegations were submitted to the U.S. Office of Special Counsel (OSC), if that agency found a "substantial likelihood" that he was illegally fired, the USDA would be required by law to investigate his charges and issue a report. (While the OSC was established to investigate claims of reprisals against federal whistleblowers and to provide whistleblowers with a safe mechanism to disclose government corruption, that office almost never finds sufficient evidence to warrant further investigation of whistleblowers' complaints.)

To our surprise, the OSC ruled in Walker's favor and the USDA sent two supervisors to Kaplan to conduct a review. Instead of questioning Walker or any of his fellow brucellosis testers, however, the reviewers conducted a forewarned tour of the plant one morning, did a little poking around, and interviewed a few plant workers who were not free to speak.

According to the *Tampa Tribune,* Kaplan was one of the biggest beef packers in the southeast United States, had annual sales of close to seventy million dollars, and had planned to expand its operation. Still, days after the USDA's shoddy review was conducted, but before the findings were released, Kaplan Industries mysteriously stopped operations and went out of business. Two hundred and sixty workers were informed of a problem with the plant's boiler and, without notice or severance pay, were permanently laid off.

Two months after the USDA's investigation—and shortly *after* the plant closed its doors—then Secretary of Agriculture Edward Madigan issued the findings of the USDA's investigation into Walker's charges. The secretary gave Kaplan a glowing report, glossing over all fourteen of Walker's allegations, and declaring each one unfounded. "Based upon the findings of the inquiry," summarized the secretary, "it is our conclusion that USDA officials assigned to the establishment have enforced the Humane Slaughter Act."

After all the USDA corruption I'd encountered, this was the most brazen so far. This wasn't some midlevel supervisor at the USDA instigating a coverup. This was the highest-ranking agriculture official in the country, a member of the Cabinet, answerable only to the president of the United States, signing off on a document riddled with lies.

※　※　※

Next, under the Whistleblower Protection Act, Walker was given one last opportunity to refute the secretary's findings in writing. While the plant's sudden closing precluded any further investigations, little did USDA officials know that we'd already amassed a mountain of evidence that irrefutably supported all fourteen of Walker's claims. Thus, in his written rebuttal to the secretary's report, Walker was able to present the agency with thirty-five pages of excerpts from testimony documenting the inaccuracies in the secretary's five-page report.

But that wasn't all Walker was able to do. In his rebuttal, we were also able to demonstrate that the secretary of agriculture, in an attempt to defend the USDA, had unwittingly documented that the USDA was violating the law.

When answering Walker's charge that falling animals threatened USDA personnel, the secretary of agriculture claimed such hazards weren't a concern to the USDA because the "area adjacent to the knocking box where the stunned animals are hoisted to the overhead rail . . . is not an area where inspectors perform their tasks." As for the charge that floors covered with coagulated blood and animal parts posed a threat to agency personnel, this too was not a problem because "the blood pit is not a working area for USDA employees." And when addressing an allegation that the pneumatic dehorner—an air-driven jawlike tool with two dangerously sharp blades—posed a risk to workers on the cramped catwalk, the secretary dismissed the complaint, stating, "Again, since no USDA employees worked at this location, the operation of the machine did not present a hazard to employees."

If inspectors were permitted to enforce the HSA, the agriculture secretary left us wondering where they would position themselves since the stunning, shackling, and sticking areas were all forbidden ground. In his attempt to defend the USDA, the secretary had not only undermined his entire defense but had built a strong case as to why inspectors could not enforce the Humane Slaughter Act.

"The fact that the areas where animals were being killed were considered off-limits to inspectors," read Walker's rebuttal, "only confirms my allegations that humane regulations were not being enforced at Kaplan.

"At the time of my initial complaint a USDA official admitted to investigator Eisnitz that, due to the plant's reputation as an outdated facility, she wouldn't have been surprised if my allegations were true. Yet, in the secretary's findings, Kaplan is portrayed as a model plant for all slaughter establishments to emulate."

Walker and I were looking forward to using the public hearing that would follow as a media hook to publicize slaughterhouse violations. Instead, nearly two years after firing Walker, USDA officials took one look at his rebuttal and, to avoid a highly embarrassing administrative appeal, offered Walker an impressive package to settle his case out-of-court. Not only would they rehire Walker and expunge all records of his termination, but they would give him a retroactive promotion, back pay, vacation and sick time, and relocation expenses.

Walker wanted to fight on to expose slaughterhouse conditions, but GAP was understandably thrilled with the victory. Walker—who, since being fired by the USDA, had been shunned by all prospective employers—accepted the settlement.

There was once an ad for the movie *Alien* that said, "In space no one can hear you scream." Well, in a vacuum of media coverage, no one can hear you win. Timothy Walker had his career back, but the animals were no better off and the meat industry was no closer to reform.

PART FIVE

FRIENDS IN HIGH PLACES

20

Almost Dying for a Cause

By this time, I felt like my body was falling apart. I couldn't swallow, breathe, or sleep, and was doubled over with stomach cramps.

One morning, after being up most of the night, I crawled out of bed and into the shower and began lathering myself with soap. My fingers took a little hiccup over a bump I hadn't noticed before. I checked it out again, slowly and carefully. I had a lump in my breast.

*　*　*

I was so accustomed to taking care of myself, I went for the lumpectomy alone. Once I was sedated, the surgeon would remove the suspicious lump from my breast, and a biopsy would reveal whether it had been cancerous or not. The doctor had put me on standby for outpatient surgery about a week after I'd found the lump. So there I sat in the crowded hospital waiting room for four long hours awaiting my turn. All the women around me were accompanied by husbands and friends.

An hour after surgery, stitched up and groggy from the sedative, I made my way to the surgeon's office in the building across the street. The doctor had told me that he wouldn't know the results of the biopsy that day but, for some unknown reason, he had still requested a consultation with me.

The surgeon ushered me into his office and explained that he'd rushed my lump through the lab. "Please have a seat," he said, motioning me to the big leather chair across from his desk.

I was completely unaware of the gravity of the situation, never for a moment believing I would be sick.

"It's cancer," he said.

* * *

I was broadsided with a wave of fatigue. As I sat, it took every ounce of energy I had just to stay awake. All I wanted to do was get home, crawl into my safe little bed, and pull the covers over my head.

The doctor drew diagrams and pointed at them. His mouth was moving, sound was coming out as if from far away. He was looking at me. He asked me something. I nodded and smiled, then got up and walked out.

The surgeon called me the next afternoon. The cancer appeared limited to the one area and had not spread throughout my body. For the next six months I'd undergo chemotherapy, have chemicals injected into me that would eradicate any remaining cancer cells. Radiation, which would take about six weeks, would involve a daily trip to the hospital. A huge X-ray machine would irradiate the area where the lump had been.

A doctor drew large colorful Xs on my breast, targets for the radiation beam. This type of treatment would allow me to save my breast completely intact, miraculously unscathed. My long blonde hair would probably fall out, but I could handle that.

＊　＊　＊

I proceeded with my investigation, scheduling trips to slaughterhouses in between chemo treatments. My oncologist said he'd never known anyone like me: I was the only patient he'd had who carried a cooler on board airplanes filled with syringes of high-priced serum which I had to self-inject to boost my immune system.

I was in a strange Midwest town to meet with more informants when suddenly I felt particularly ill. I stopped in a cancer clinic filled with farmers and their wives. I was the only person under age fifty, and felt very out of place. My skin hurt; my chemo-irritated eyes felt like they were burning out of my head; my lungs, scorched during radiation, made it painful to inhale. The doctor said that my immune system was so compromised from chemo that if my fever reached 101° F, I would have to check myself immediately into the local hospital. I'd faxed the results of tests to my oncologist back home, but he'd misread them and never called me back.

That night I lay on my motel room bed, thermometer in mouth. I had no energy, my pulse was pounding in my bones. When I looked at the thermometer, it read 100.6°. Another four-tenths of a degree and it would be off to the hospital for me. The thought kept crossing my mind about how sad it would be to die in this unfamiliar town. I had visions of my parents and sister flying to the Midwest only to say good-bye to me in this far-off place.

A half hour went by and another look at the thermometer: 100.7°. I prepared myself mentally for the trip to the hospital. And then, I could barely keep from checking my temperature every minute or so. I felt like an out-of-luck gambler hoping to win back her life's savings on one last bet.

My fever peaked at around 100.8°, then very gradually dropped. The next day, it was business as usual for me, as I tried to document violations at the plant.

※　※　※

On another trip I found myself in a hospital emergency room in another unfamiliar town. I was having such difficulty inhaling that the doctor feared I might have a blood clot in my lungs, an uncommon—but potentially fatal—side effect of chemotherapy. It was Sunday morning and a pulmonary specialist in this sleepy Great Plains town was called into the hospital to have a look at me. He put me on a gurney and wheeled me into an examining room. He took a porcelain syringe out of an insulated cabinet bearing the three-triangle symbol for radioactive materials. As if I didn't already have enough radiation in me, the specialist told me to inhale the substance as deep as I possibly could.

Luckily for me, no blood clot was found. In fact, no doctor was ever able to tell me what the problem had been. Shortly thereafter, I felt a little better, and found myself investigating again.

❈   ❈   ❈

I received a complaint from workers in California that hogs at their plant were not being properly stunned. By now, I was so depleted from chemo and radiation that I could barely stay awake. Still, wearing my trusty wig covering the few remaining wisps of hair on my head, I headed out West.

It was a plant where squealing hogs were left straddling the restrainer and dangling live by one leg when workers left the stick pit for their half-hour lunch breaks; where stunners were shocking hogs three and four times; where inadequately stunned hogs were jumping from the shackling table into the blood pit below, smashing into metal pipes on the trip down and fracturing legs and backs; where whether broken or not, thousands of squealing hogs were immersed in the plant's scalding tank alive.

21

In Bed with a Bird

It was time to take my investigation to the next phase. Both lines of inquiry—contaminated meat and animal cruelty—had led from the slaughterhouses to the inspectors to the veterinarians, and then disappeared up into the executive strata of the USDA. I decided to do some more research.

✻   ✻   ✻

The National Cattlemen's Association (NCA) called her "Ms. President." The *Washington Post* dubbed her the "First Lady of American Agriculture." The Bush administration called her "Ms. Assistant Secretary." But it was the *Kansas City Star* that said it best, calling her "the nation's top meat inspector" and declaring her position at the USDA "a textbook conflict of interest case."

It all began in the 1970s when JoAnn Smith, a fifth-generation cattle rancher, began climbing the ranks within the National Cattlemen's Association, a Denver-based organization representing 230,000 ranchers. After chairing the group's beef promotion committee, serving as representative to the National Live Stock and Meat Board, and being elected vice president, Smith was appointed the organization's first female president in 1985.*

"I am convinced that our job is to express the positive story about beef," Smith said in her NCA presidential acceptance speech. "That's great, because that's what I do best." When not lobbying Congress and testifying on behalf of the cattlemen's interests, "the first woman to represent the $30 billion beef industry," as the *New York Times* called her, spent her term traveling the country and giving speeches and media interviews. Determined to resurrect a faltering market by enhancing the public's perception of beef, Smith aggressively promoted beef consumption wherever she went. "No cattleman ever received the publicity that Smith did," reported the NCA's membership magazine. "She appeared in prime time on all three television networks. Broadcasters and newspaper reporters were waiting at almost every stop she made. The total value of the print and air time she received has been estimated at $8 to $10 million."

The total value of Smith's efforts was more likely in the range of hundreds of millions of dollars. It was Smith who led a decade-long legislative campaign that culminated, during her

---

*In 1996, the National Cattlemen's Association and National Live Stock and Meat Board merged to form the National Cattlemen's Beef Association.

NCA presidency, with Congress's passage of a national beef checkoff. Under that legislation, ranchers must contribute one dollar to the Cattlemen's Beef Promotion and Research Board (or Beef Board) for every head of cattle they sell. The Beef Board and its authorized state beef councils then spend most of the $79 million raised each year on advertisements promoting the consumption of beef. In 1986, following her term as NCA president, Smith was elected the first chairman of the Beef Board, where she invested millions of dollars in promotional campaigns based on the now-famous slogan "Beef. Real Food for Real People."

To summarize, she'd worked as a rancher, PR consultant, lobbyist, spokeswoman, and policy maker to the meat industry. Hailed the industry's most effective voice for beef consumption, she had devoted her entire career to convincing Americans to eat more beef. Thus, with the American Meat Institute—the meat industry's trade association—rallying behind her, Smith was appointed the Bush administration's Assistant Secretary of Agriculture for Marketing and Inspection Services in May 1989.

Would the beef industry's top spokesperson, an individual whose life's goal was to increase beef consumption, really make an appropriate candidate as the nation's chief watchdog ensuring compliance with regulations in federally inspected plants?

According to the *Kansas City Star,* one of Assistant Secretary Smith's first actions, at the request of the National Cattlemen's Association, was to authorize the use of leftover tidbits of beef trimmings and cartilage and then allow them to be labeled as meat. By separating these morsels from beef byproducts and then allowing them to be included in beef patties, she was enhancing the carcass value of beef as much as seven dollars a head—a decision worth millions of dollars annually to the beef industry.

I went to see Rodney Leonard, who had served as the USDA's Director of Food Inspection in the Johnson administration and now heads the Community Nutrition Institute in Washington, D.C.

"Fat-reduced beef isn't meat," he explained. "It's fatty tissue, the solid part of fat. It's a gray, ugly mass. It makes you sick to look at it. They form it into patties, color it, freeze it—if you leave it out too long it will start to smell—and then they tell you to cook it."

"It's connective tissue that contains high levels of proteins that your body cannot use," said Dr. Jack Leighty, a former USDA veterinarian and an associate of Leonard's. "The protein in fat-reduced beef is useless. It's like adding water or sand to the meat product."

"Everybody in industry knows that it's a perfect forum for breeding bacteria," added Rod Leonard. "The fact that two years after JoAnn Smith became assistant secretary you had all of these outbreaks of bacteria—they're directly attributable to that kind of disregard of health issues."*

---

*Fat-reduced beef is not unlike other "pseudomeats," as Rod Leonard calls them, products that, had the definition of meat not been stretched for the benefit of the meat industry, would have otherwise gone to rendering. Advanced Meat Recovery (AMR), for instance, is a recently approved process whereby particles of tissue are separated from bone through the use of high pressure technology. AMR meat is then included in ground beef. Recent studies have documented that AMR meat contains excess bone marrow and spinal cord tissue. Because spinal tissue appears to be a mechanism of transmission of Mad Cow-like diseases (transmissible spongiform encephalopathies), the inclusion of spinal cords in hamburgers subjects consumers to yet another unnecessary risk.

※ ※ ※

The controversial nature of Smith's appointment at the USDA wasn't limited to the assistant secretary alone. "Congress has assigned USDA two radically opposing missions," explained GAP's Tom Devine over the phone. "The very same officials who are charged with promoting the sale of agricultural products are also supposed to protect the consumers from filth and unscrupulous practices." As a result of the USDA's duplicitous mandate and its primary focus on marketing, the department's ranks have long been filled with industry leaders who have demonstrated their abilities at increasing industry profits.

"USDA is unsurpassed as a historical example of the regulated industry formally policing itself from inside the government," Devine said. "The department has the crudest revolving door in the executive branch." In fact, as far back as 1983, author Kathleen Hughes wrote *Return to the Jungle,* an exposé of the collusive partnership forged between the Reagan administration and the meat industry. By that time, Ronald Reagan had already appointed three agribusiness leaders to head up the USDA: the secretary of agriculture was John Block, a corporate hog producer from Illinois; the assistant secretary—later to become the secretary—was Richard Lyng, president of the American Meat Institute; and the assistant secretary for Marketing and Inspection Services was William McMillan, a former meat-packing executive and vice president of the National Cattlemen's Association. Once these officials were placed in positions of such influence, the industry was virtually running the USDA.

And the trend has continued to this day. Dr. Lester Crawford, the head of the USDA's meat inspection program from

1987 to 1991, left his USDA post to accept a position as executive vice president for the National Food Processors Association. Dr. H. Russell Cross, whom JoAnn Smith chose to replace Crawford, was revered by the regulated industry and endorsed by the American Meat Institute for the job. Cross, a department head at Texas A&M and an expert in the production of low-fat beef—not in public health—had previously headed up a beef industry-financed project designed to convince consumers and the USDA that beef was leaner than they thought.

During his tenure at the USDA, Cross continued his term as a trustee in the Livestock Industry Institute, an organization which aims to increase profits within the red meat industry. According to the *Los Angeles Times* he also maintained the same salary he had at Texas A&M, and retained benefits and tenure from the university while the university was getting millions of dollars in contracts from the USDA to run its training program for USDA inspectors.

"Here's a guy who built a program at Texas A&M," Rod Leonard said. "He got the financing for it from the meat industry. He identified himself as a Republican and said, in effect, that he thoroughly supported the party's objective of deregulating the inspection program." Still, with the support of some key members of Congress and some of the country's most powerful agribusiness interests, the USDA official known to the beef industry as "our man in D.C." was retained by the Clinton administration.

"Why did the Democrats keep him?" I asked.

"USDA has always been an industry-run operation," Leonard replied. "With the Clinton administration, we held out the hope that there would be a change. Unfortunately, Secretary Mike Espy did nothing to change the basic focus of the program. In fact, the most significant act that Secretary Espy took was to retain Dr. Cross. What Espy was planning to do was to maintain the status quo. He was carrying out the policies of the Reagan and Bush administrations."

Just why would a Democratic administration carry out the deregulatory policies of the Reagan and Bush administrations? I spent the next few days at the library.

Don Tyson, the senior chairman of the board of Tyson Foods of Arkansas—the world's largest poultry processor* and one of the nation's leading seafood and pork producers—maintains close ties to the White House. In addition to being a longtime Clinton friend, Tyson was also the second-largest contributor to a $220,000 fund that Clinton used to pursue his Arkansas political agenda.

During his governorship, Bill Clinton had courted the huge Arkansas poultry industry in an effort to create jobs for his state. While he was able to claim Arkansas as number one in job creation during his bid for the presidency, according to *Time* magazine, "Clinton has shown the trade-offs he would be willing to make." These trade-offs ranged from deplorable working conditions and low wages for poultry workers and contract growers to environmental disasters for the state's residents.

Governor Clinton, *Time* said, showered "the largest chicken producer, Tyson Foods, with millions of dollars in tax breaks for expanding its plants and workforce," and provided other development incentives as well. What's more, state regulators under Clinton took a relaxed attitude toward enforcement of the state's environmental regulations, permitting the poultry industry to

---

*The only entities producing more chicken than Tyson Foods are the countries of Brazil and China.

pollute hundreds of miles of rivers, streams, and groundwater with chicken feces and contaminated water.

"The boom years for Tyson paralleled Clinton's time as a governor consumed with the cause of economic growth for his rural, impoverished state," said the *Washington Post*. According to annual reports, Tyson revenues skyrocketed from $604 million in 1983—shortly after Clinton became governor of Arkansas—to $4.7 billion in 1993 when Clinton left the governor's office for the White House.

"The Tyson-Clinton connection stands out even in a department long faulted for a tendency to accommodate agribusiness interests," the *Wall Street Journal* reported in 1994. Tyson chief attorney James B. Blair, for instance, a longtime Clinton friend and confidant, was dubbed "The Man Clinton Turns to in Times of Turmoil" by the *New York Times*. He was also the guiding force behind Hillary Clinton's 1979 windfall in which she turned a thousand-dollar investment in cattle futures into nearly one hundred thousand dollars. Blair's wife, Diane, a political scientist, served as a top advisor to Clinton during his presidential campaign. The Blairs were overnight guests at the White House the night of the 1993 Clinton inauguration.

"Don Tyson, meanwhile, has been a loyal Clinton backer for years, flying him around Arkansas on Tyson aircraft and picking up the tab for many meals." The *Wall Street Journal* went on to tally the contributions Tyson executives and family members made to Clinton's presidential campaign, and reported that Tyson even made a sizable contribution to Secretary Espy's brother in 1993 during his unsuccessful bid for Congress.

And just what did Tyson get in return from the Clinton administration? "A year ago, department officials were working on a policy for the poultry industry that would have sharply tightened requirements to trim off, rather than wash off, badly contaminated flesh, wings or legs," the *Wall Street Journal* said. The policy, intended to reduce salmonella poisoning, would have resulted in slower line speeds and more poultry being condemned.

"But [USDA] officials say that they were told by Mr. Espy's office to drop the proposal and that an Espy aide ordered them to turn over all evidence of their work, including information on computers." Espy and his staff then proposed a new set of regulations that would have reduced the number of on-line inspectors in over half of the nation's poultry plants.

Secretary Espy, who, according to the *Wall Street Journal,* admitted meeting with Tyson lobbyists "all the time," eventually became the subject of a major investigation by the Department of Justice and Congress about the illegal gifts and trips he received from Tyson. In October 1994, Espy was forced to resign his post.

In August 1997, Mike Espy was indicted by a federal grand jury for illegally accepting gifts worth tens of thousands of dollars from food companies associated with the USDA. According to the 39-count indictment, Espy allegedly committed mail and wire fraud, violated the Federal Meat Inspection Act by accepting gifts worth more than $35,000 from the regulated industry, lied to the FBI and other investigating agencies, and tampered with a witness when he instructed a USDA staff member to alter a document requested by investigators. According to the indictment, he allegedly accepted such gifts as luggage, crystal, airfare, and trips from seven major companies.

In December 1998, Espy was acquitted of the charges. However, two agribusiness lobbyists—one of them a Tyson lobbyist—were convicted of lying to FBI agents when questioned about their involvement in the gift-giving activities. Tyson's director of governmental affairs was also convicted of providing illegal gifts to Espy on two occasions with intent to influence the Secretary. He now faces a year in prison on each of the two counts. Tyson Foods also pleaded guilty to providing illegal gratuities to Espy while the company had business before the USDA and was fined a total of $6 million. Espy's former chief of staff was convicted of lying to conceal payments from farming associates and sentenced to serve 27 months in prison. Another major agribusiness corporation was fined $1.5 million by the US District Court, Washington, DC for making illegal gifts to Secretary Espy and illegal campaign contributions to the secretary's brother, and a third was fined $100,000 for illegal gift-giving. In all, the investigation into gifts received by Secretary Espy generated 16 convictions and $11 million in fines.*

----

*Secretary Espy's untimely departure put former Kansas Congressman Daniel Glickman at the USDA's helm. As a career politician, his ties to the meat and poultry industries were limited. Even so, as a member of the House Agriculture Committee, he had helped push through legislation that allowed a major pizza restaurant chain to sell meat-topped pizza to the school lunch program without going through normal inspection required by federal law. (Foods going into the school lunch program must be federally inspected during processing to ensure that they haven't become contaminated during handling.)

Despite the potential impact on the health of schoolchildren, then Congressman Glickman avoided hearings on the issue by declaring the move a technical change. "He used that as a device to benefit a huge corporation," explained Rodney Leonard, "and, he endangered the health of schoolchildren all across the country." The move was a windfall, however, for the pizza chain, headquartered in Glickman's congressional district.

Michael Taylor, Glickman's first undersecretary for meat inspection, brought conflicts of his own from his former position as deputy commissioner for policy at the Food and Drug Administration (FDA). According to a 1994 *New York Times* story, three members of Congress charged that Taylor and two others may have "collaborated with the manufacturer of a genetically engineered dairy hormone in clearing the new hormone for sale." (The drug, Bovine Growth Hormone, is used to increase milk production and has known side effects in cows and suspected ones in human consumers.) Taylor had originally left a post at the FDA to work for the Washington law firm that represented the hormone manufacturer in its efforts to obtain FDA approval. Despite this, Taylor ultimately returned to the FDA where he developed the agency's formal policy that the highly controversial drug was safe, should be approved, and did not require special labeling.

22

The Lesson

As I'd found out when I started this investigation, USDA officials all the way to Washington knew that conditions at Kaplan Industries in Florida were substandard. Only when required by the federal Whistleblower Protection Act did the USDA conduct an investigation of its own. Then, before the secretary of agriculture issued his specious report, all evidence of department improprieties at Kaplan was destroyed. And thus, Florida's largest beef slaughterhouse abruptly closed its doors.

Not only had Assistant Secretary of Agriculture JoAnn Smith's family raised cattle for five generations, but the family's cow-calf ranch was located in north central Florida. She'd served on several cattle advisory boards throughout Florida, had received every accolade the Florida Cattlemen's Association and the Florida Department of Agriculture could give her, been named Farm Wife of the Year and Outstanding Woman in Florida Agriculture. Her husband had served as chairman of the Florida Beef Council and later as president of the Florida Cattlemen's Association.

I called the Gainesville Livestock Market, the auction house closest to the Smith ranch.

"This probably sounds weird, but I'd really like to buy a cow from the former Assistant Agriculture Secretary JoAnn Smith," I said. "Do you handle her cows?"

"Used to, up until about a year ago," he said. "They're not ranching right now."

"Darn. Can I ask you another question?"

"Sure," he said in a friendly tone.

"Did an outfit called Kaplan ever buy from you?"

"Sure they did," he said. "Why?"

"Did they ever buy any of JoAnn Smith's cows?"

"Imagine so. *Buyers for Kaplan bought the bulk of our cows.*"

※   ※   ※

She had built her reputation promoting beef; she was a former industry spokeswoman; a marketing whiz whose ambition was to enhance the public's perception of beef. More importantly, she was the nation's chief meat inspector, the senior-most official at the USDA directly responsible for enforcing the Humane Slaughter Act.

Suddenly there was a strong possibility that cows from her ranch had been slaughtered at Kaplan's packing plant. Just what would a revelation like that have done to Smith and the USDA, not to mention the beef industry to which she was so closely tied? What would have happened had the public gotten wind that the assistant secretary's own cattle—in a plant under her authority—had not been adequately stunned or stuck, and had had their heads skinned while they were still alive?

※   ※   ※

After six months, my chemotherapy drew to a welcome end. My hair started to grow back, shiny and even thicker than before. Along with my beautiful new hair came a new perspective on life. I'd felt that my investigation into slaughterhouses had been making me emotionally dead, inuring me to the suffering of the animals I was trying to help. What I'd missed entirely was that I'd long ago become emotionally dead toward everything *but* the animals.

It was as if for the first time in my life, cancer had given me a reason to put myself first, to take care of myself, to treat myself with love. It was not exactly the way I would've chosen to educate myself, but it was an invaluable lesson, and one I truly needed to learn.

※   ※   ※

Shortly after my treatment, I read in magazines and watched on NBC's "Tonight Show" as a winner of a Seattle contest demonstrated his unique skill. It was an annual event held during Seattle's Fat Tuesday Celebration, in which eighty-five contestants were given fifteen minutes to show off their carving skills. The entrants were not provided wood or clay. Rather, they were each given two twelve-ounce cans of Spam into which they were supposed to carve.

According to *People* magazine, which reported the results of the annual "Spam Speed-Carving Contest," the event's intention was to "expand the creative boundaries of ground ham, pork shoulder, salt, sugar, water and sodium nitrate." And in the words of one contestant, "It's tough to get smooth cuts with all those tiny red blobs."

According to the contest winner, who demonstrated on the "Tonight Show" how to craft crude animal figures out of Spam (a commercial trademarked product of the Hormel company), carving up animal flesh for entertainment "felt like the natural thing to do." While he was busy disassociating himself from the fact that the material he was carving into had once been alive, I was left wondering what the slaughterhouse circumstances were under which it had died.

Just what does it say about society when network entertainment execs refuse to expose violations of federal laws? Instead, they provide time to teach an audience of tens of millions how to carve miniature animals out of processed animal flesh. What I wouldn't have done to have gotten those eleven minutes of airtime to expose slaughterhouse violations.

※   ※   ※

During the early stages of my investigation, I'd been engaged in a battle even more frustrating and personal than the one I was waging with the networks. The very people I most needed support from were putting roadblocks in my path.

For years I'd worked for an organization called the Humane Society of the United States (HSUS). Shortly after I began my slaughter investigation, however, a new vice president was hired by the HSUS.

My new supervisor focused on splashy, symbolic animal issues that brought him airtime and column space in the print media. In the meantime, he instructed me not to speak to the media and attempted to undermine the slaughterhouse investigation by depriving it of funds. While this vice president was traveling around the world wining and dining on HSUS's tab, I was defiantly continuing to provide my documentation to the media, and futilely pleading with his supervisors at HSUS to support the investigation.

The last straw came when my supervisor announced that, henceforth, to generate media attention, we were only to initiate high-profile investigations that could be completed in eleven days. This made in-depth investigations next to impossible. I knew the only way I could ever continue to document and expose slaughter violations would be to resign.*

I applied for a job at the Humane Farming Association (HFA), the nation's largest organization dedicated to protecting farm animals. Based in San Francisco, HFA had established an impressive reputation as an organization that had accomplished a great deal on behalf of farm animals. HFA's national veal

---

*That supervisor was later fired from the HSUS for falsifying his expense reports. In June, 1998, he was criminally indicted by a Maryland grand jury for embezzling nearly $90,000 from the society. In June, 1999, he pleaded guilty to one count in Maryland Circuit Court, and agreed to make partial restitution and serve a six-month jail term. He also admitted in a *Washington Post* cover story to having faked his resumé and altered his academic record to mask time spent in jail for a 1973 burglarly conviction. (The *Washington Post*, June 13, 1998, p. C7; The *Washington Post*, June 17, 1999, p. B2.)

boycott, for instance, is widely regarded as the most successful farm animal campaign ever conducted in the United States. Similarly, the organization's efforts against genetically engineered Bovine Growth Hormone had been pivotal in mobilizing the public against that dangerous drug. And HFA has led the charge against the factory farming of chickens, pigs, and other farm animals

I'd always figured that if I ever left HSUS, the Humane Farming Association would be the place I'd want to go. In contrast to my former employer, HFA's National Director Bradley Miller was eager to provide me the means to continue documenting slaughter violations. I was delighted and relieved to have found an organization that truly cared.

Miller is a very down-to-earth, no nonsense kind of guy. If the media doesn't have the incentive to expose animal exploitation, then he sees to it that HFA does the job itself. For years, HFA had been running highly effective full-page national magazine and newspaper advertisements to inform America about factory farm animal abuses and threats to human health.

Similarly, Miller thought that if no TV executive had the courage to air the slaughterhouse abuses HFA had helped me document, then we should simply tell the story ourselves. If the networks felt no social obligation to inform Americans of government corruption and animal abuse, he said, then it becomes our responsibility to do just that. And that's when, at his suggestion, I started to write this book.

PART SIX

A DEBASED SIDE OF HUMAN NATURE

23

America's Premier Hog Kill

John Morrell's slaughterhouses in Iowa and South Dakota were purchased by Smithfield Foods, Inc., a huge agribusiness conglomerate headquartered in Norfolk, Virginia and now the country's number-one producer of pork products. Its new state-of-the-art plant, Carolina Food Processors (Carolina Foods) in Bladen County, North Carolina, was killing 144,000 pigs *a week,* and had requested a permit to increase its slaughter rate to 192,000. Carolina Foods was said to be clean and well run. The animal chutes and ramps in the slaughter-house, I'd heard, had been specially designed for minimal fear and suffering. Could things at last be changing?

※　　※　　※

I went to Bladen County.

The first thing I noticed about Carolina Foods was the coverage it was getting in the local press. According to the *Raleigh News and Observer,* the community was up in arms because the plant was sucking the water table dry. The U.S. Geologic Survey had reported a 90-foot drop in the underground aquifer in just two years. In the meantime, reported *The State* (Columbia, South Carolina), millions of gallons of wastewater were pouring from the factory into a major river, and the town often reeked of burned animal flesh and hog manure. According to *The Robesonian* (Robeson County, North Carolina), the hiring of Hispanic workers had put a strain on social service programs and so many employees had been injured at the plant that a law firm had opened an area office to discuss workers' compensation claims. Smithfield CEO Joseph W. Luter III was referred to locally by environmental activists as Luter the Polluter. And the company's Virginia plants were under investigation by state and federal authorities for a possible 5,000 counts of Clean Water Act violations.*

A reporter gave me the names of some Carolina Foods workers.

---

*In August 1997, Smithfield Foods was convicted in federal court and fined $12.6 million for what ultimately turned out to be nearly 7,000 counts of illegally discharging hog plant wastes into a major Virginia waterway and then falsifying records to cover up its activities. The $12.6 million fine is the largest Clean Water Act penalty in history. Meanwhile, the Commonwealth of Virginia has filed a separate suit against the company alleging 22,000 pollution violations since 1986.

✳   ✳   ✳

Carol Reynolds, an attractive African-American woman in her mid-forties, lived with her husband and four sons in a tiny old house in the country. She worked in ' casings," where manure was cleaned out of the animals' intestines so they could be used in sausage and chitlin production.

While Reynolds explained that she'd never visited the pens or the blood pit, she spoke at length about what it was like to work at the plant. She told me how acid from the hogs' intestines splashed and burned permanent holes in her skin: how "any intestines, even human intestines have acid. Whether it's battery acid or intestinal acid, it's going to eat you up.

"Eventually, they let me go to the nurse's station four times a day to get my arms re-wrapped because they knew the shit was eating me up," she said. She told me how working the same muscle thousands of times a day caused her hands to swell. Her feet were so swollen from standing on concrete for ten hours a day, "I used to stuff maybe seven of those little [sanitary] cotton hats [we wear] inside each boot just so I could stand."

"So there's still feces in the hogs' intestines when they come to you?" I asked her.

"Yeah!" she said. "And nine times out of ten those hogs have roundworms as long as this table here. And they curl up. I mean, I fish, but they're not white worms.

"Anyway, I don't mind doing the job. But my boss would bring big handfuls of worms and they would be stringing like spaghetti. He'd say, 'See, Carol. If you just touch them, you'll be over your fear.'

"I said, 'Get in my face with them and I'm going to scald you.' Because that's how big these worms were.

"I don't buy Smithfield pork. I mean, you go work where you've got twelve-inch roundworms hanging on your foot as you're walking and you're dragging these worms. Are you going to get up in the morning and fry some bacon? Or sausage? Could be ground-up worms making that sausage."

* * *

Both Betty Jane Stephens and her daughter Alcie worked at the plant. I sat and talked with them in the kitchen of their small, immaculate house. Betty Jane explained that she now worked assembling cardboard boxes; Alcie had recently been transferred from chitlins to cutting up meat.

"I've heard quite a few stories, but we never go down to where they kill them," said Betty Jane, a gray-haired woman in her sixties. "If it's anything like what I've seen, I'm sure the stories are true."

"What *have* you seen?" I asked.

"Well," Alcie, who was in her thirties, began, "for starters, they exploit Hispanic workers because they can't really speak out. They hire a lot of illegals, too. Some are just children— twelve and thirteen, maybe fourteen years old."

"One little boy couldn't speak English," added Betty Jane, "and they gave him a smock big enough for a six-foot tall man. He couldn't work with his hands in the sleeves so I rolled them up and put rubber bands on them. His little arms were about this big," she said, making a circle with her thumb and forefinger the size of a silver dollar.

Hiring illegal aliens has several advantages: they don't report their injuries, they don't have any recourse if they get hurt or fired, they don't unionize, and they're willing to work for low wages. After working for the Mexican minimum wage of three dollars a day, seven dollars an hour offered by packers seems like big bucks.

"And then there are the inmates," said Alcie. She described the North Carolina Correction Department work-release program in which violent criminal offenders are sent to Carolina Foods to work directly with the employees.

"Unsupervised," added Betty Jane. "And most of them are in jail for rape, murder, robbery, you name it. There was one prisoner I worked with," she continued, "I found out that he had murdered one woman, raped and murdered another. I read about it in the *Bladen Journal* after he escaped—after he walked away from the plant one day.

"Another guy I work with killed a sixteen-year-old boy and damaged another one for life. He told me they were trying to rob him, but he shot both of them in the back."

"They wear prison uniforms, don't they?" I asked.

"Some of them wear prison clothes, and some of them wear their own clothes," Betty Jane replied.

"Do they use knives?" I asked.

"Sure they do," replied Betty Jane. "They use stabbing knives."

"So, Alcie," I asked, "what was it like working in chitlins?"

"You're working in manure all day. You're piping the manure out of the gut," she replied. "My arm stayed swelled up every day for eight months until they transferred me out. Some days it would be swelled up from the tips of my fingers all the way up to my shoulder. And I smelled terrible every day."

"I worked on the cut floor [deboning meat]," Betty Jane added as she stood up. "They gave us knives to use, but didn't give us any instructions in how to use them to keep our hands from gettin' sore." She left the room momentarily and reappeared carrying something.

"Now this is what I have to sleep with every night," she said, showing me her splints. "First the numbness kicks in around midnight, then the pain gets so bad I have to get up no matter what time it is. But the company doctor says everybody comes there with carpal tunnel, that you can get it from washing dishes or hoeing tobacco. Well, I would've had to wash enough dishes to go from here to New York to get my hands in this shape. And if I got it when I hoed tobacco, I haven't hoed tobacco in twenty years."

"What's the worst thing that's happened to you there?" I asked Betty Jane.

"Gettin' that job," she sighed. "Acceptin' that job was the worst mistake I ever made."

＊　＊　＊

Carol Reynolds had given me a name of a guy who worked driving hogs through the chutes. Perhaps he knew what was going on in the blood pit.

The man sounded a bit disoriented when I called him, but agreed to meet with me. I got directions from his brother Robert and set off.

I followed Robert's directions down backwoods dirt roads for an hour or more, stopping three or four times at tumbledown houses to ask where I was. Finally I arrived at the farm I was looking for, not a factory farm but a real farm with pigs out in the fields. There were four or five houses on it and kids running from house to house.

I found Robert and asked for his brother.

"He left to go partying somewhere," Robert said.

"But he knew I was coming all the way out here to see him," I said.

Robert shrugged half in apology, half in resignation. I stood there arms crossed, teeth clenched to stop myself from cursing out his brother to his face.

"Tell you what," he said. "Let's go see my cousin."

We walked across the yard to another house. A car was running in the driveway, and when we got closer I could see a big black man sitting behind the wheel. As we walked up, he rolled down the passenger window and looked at us with sorrowful eyes.

"This is my cousin Nathan Price," Robert said. "He works at Carolina Foods. Nathan, you got time to talk to her?"

Price hesitated for a moment, then reached over and pushed open the passenger door. I thanked Robert and got into the car.

"What's your job there?" I asked him.

"Sticker," he replied.

"For how long?"

"Two and a half years."

"Does it ever happen that hogs aren't properly stunned?" I asked.

"All the time," Price laughed. "Because if you're killing 16,000 hogs a shift, those guys aren't going to stun all them hogs all the time. Some hogs come out kicking and raising hell."

"Is kicking the only sign they're not stunned properly?" I asked.

"Running across the table or floor isn't a good sign neither. See, they use this four-pronged stunner. And if you don't hit that hog precisely, that hog runs across the table."

"Does that happen often?" I asked.

"Sure," he replied. "Because most of the time those stunners are not getting the right charge to connect to the hog. Then, if a person can knock that hog down without stunning it and put a shackle around it, they're going to hang that hog up.

"If a hog ain't stunned correctly, then the shackler's supposed to let it hit the floor and somebody else is supposed to restun that hog and hang him up."

He spoke politely and deliberately, as if he had to force out each word. "But the supervisors don't want the shacklers to do that. They want the shacklers to try to shackle the hog, hang it up, and keep on going. But, if the shackler drops too many hogs, they write that shackler up. A shackler out there don't have no choice *but* to hang hogs alive in order to keep his job and everything else going smooth."

"And you stick them like that?"

"Yeah," he answered. "Or, if a hog comes out kicking too much for the sticker, he's going to let him go until somebody tells him that hog needs sticking. If it's too late, and that hog hits the tub, then he goes all through the scald tank and out to the de-hairer and to the dry kill [where workers eviscerate the hogs]. And probably by that time he gets around to where they 'off' the feet and stuff, *then* they'll stick the hog. I've stuck them after they've had their hooves off, their toes split down,* and everything else.

"That hog's not stuck correctly and they should take that hog off, throw him away, and grind him up [for rendered

---

*After a hog has been scalded, its toenails (hooves) can be removed relatively easily. Then the worker makes a deep incision between the toes to expose the tendons into which meat hooks will be inserted for hanging.

product]. But they don't do that," he said. "They let the hog go on through."

"I guess unless a person falls on that line—"

"I'll tell you what," Price interrupted. "A person can fall *on* that line, *under* that line, *around* that line, *beside* that line. They don't care. They don't want that line to stop. They say, 'Bump that human and keep killing hogs.' "

"Did you ever see anybody beat hogs?" I asked.

"That's all the time," he laughed again. "You get a stubborn hog that doesn't want to go, they're going to beat that hog till he does. They use a shackle, a pipe, anything they can get their hands on.

"If the government's not around, which they're not, employees can get to beating that hog all they want to. The supervisor will not say nothing to the person. Because I have seen supervisors taking pipes and whatever they can to hit the hogs and knock them down."

"Do they ever stun them that way?"

"I've done it," he said. "Supervisors do it. But to do that, you got to hit them like you're hitting a baseball. You got to hit them across the head and knock them flat out."

Before leaving Bladen County I conducted more interviews and got Price's claims corroborated by a very reliable source at the USDA.

24

An Army of
Walking Wounded

Betty Jane Stephens had complained about carpal tunnel syndrome; her daughter Alcie had rolled up her sleeves and Carol Reynolds had lifted her shirt to show me the permanent scars that had been burned into their skin from constant exposure to acid in the hogs' intestines. And Nathan Price's expression "bump the human and keep killing hogs" played over and over in my mind.

I remembered my first visit to a slaughterhouse. I'd never seen anyone work as furiously as the men and women on that production line. Many were foreigners—Mexican, Latin American, Asian. Each performing his job so quickly—as many as ten thousand times a day—he couldn't look away for a second.*

---

*Few foreigners were willing to be interviewed. In addition to the problems posed by the language barrier, these workers were very satisfied with their wages and did not wish to jeopardize their jobs.

269

In my investigation, I'd seen the toll that increased line speeds had taken on the animals, the federal inspectors, and in the end on those who consumed the meat products. But what was the physical price exacted from employees working the line? If I was going to write a book on the subject of slaughterhouses, I was going to tell the whole story. There had been a congressional hearing in the early '90s on worker injuries in slaughterhouses. I would obtain a copy of the testimony:

"My husband was killed at the plant," testified a widow. "He was a maintenance worker and was killed when someone accidentally activated the conveyor belt he was repairing.

"OSHA cited the company for failing to provide a hazard-free workplace following my husband's death. The company was fined one thousand dollars for the death of my husband. The company contested the citation—apparently they thought this fine was too severe. My husband and I would have been married thirty-five years next month."

"The feed-out rollers accidentally became the feed-in rollers," said a beef plant worker. "When I threw the hide on the machine, the rollers pulled the hide in as well as my hand. My hand was crushed and looked like freshly ground hamburger.

"The doctor removed my glove and the top of my thumb. I was in the hospital for fifty-three days and was operated on twelve times. They sewed my thumb to my side to bring back the circulation, I looked like a mummy. My thumb was attached to my side for three weeks.

"Last week, I went to the hospital again. This time to have my hand amputated."

Another worker stated: "One time, a woman who had been complaining of headaches wasn't allowed to leave the line. She passed out and died. Maybe she died right there on the line, or maybe she hit her head when she fell. I don't know. All I know is that there was blood coming out of her eyes and ears. It was the worst thing I ever saw. Sometimes I still cry when I think about it."

"No matter how many hours we work on a workday, we have only two seven-minute breaks," said a poultry worker. "I usually have to go to the bathroom but, the bathrooms are always occupied. Breaks are the only time we are allowed to use the bathroom. Workers sometimes go to the bathroom on themselves— they have no other choice. If workers are feeling sick, they are not allowed to leave the line. Then, they get sick on the line and vomit on the floor. For pregnant workers, this problem is especially bad, but management makes no exceptions for them."

"My husband had been back to work for about a year and a half and his hand was still grossly deformed from the injury he'd gotten at the plant," said a worker's wife. "One evening, he broke down. He came downstairs to our bedroom around eleven o'clock and said he was going to do something that he might one day regret. He beat me severely for over four hours. Then he woke our two children, asked them to kiss me good-bye, that they would never see me again." After reporting him to the police and spending many weeks in a battered women's shelter, this woman divorced her husband.

✳   ✳   ✳

I phoned the Bureau of Labor Statistics and they faxed me some information. I learned that, with nearly thirty-six injuries or illnesses for every one hundred workers, meat packing is the most dangerous industry in the United States. In fact, a worker's chances of suffering an injury or an illness in a meat plant are six times greater than if that same person worked in a coal mine.

Next, I contacted GAP and asked if they'd conducted any more recent studies on hazards in meat or poultry plants.

"I was working at the plant the day a man lost his arm," stated a worker in a GAP affidavit. "A doctor from Greenville came out and cut it off at the plant. He had to, because it was embedded in the auger up to his shoulder. In my experience, two other workers had their arms torn off."

"The conditions are very dangerous," said a plant employee, "and workers aren't well trained for the machinery. One machine has a whirring blade that catches people in it. Workers lose fingers. One woman's breast got caught in it and was torn off. Another's shirt got caught and her face was dragged into it."

"Recently a young man was put on heavy machinery with only superficial training," said another. "Three hours into his first day on the job he cut off a finger. The nurse threw it in the trash, and another employee had to drive him to the hospital. To the company's credit, when the hospital asked for the finger, they went through the garbage and found it."

"I saw a man running by and yelling 'the plant is on fire,' " reported a survivor of the Imperial Foods fire in Hamlet, North Carolina, in which 25 workers were killed. "Then I saw what looked like balls of fire coming up the conveyor belt. The whole fryer [in which chickens are cooked] had burst into flames. We only had one exit. All the other doors had been locked by management because they were worried that workers would steal some chicken. I couldn't go towards that exit because the fire blocked me. I headed towards an aluminum door that the trash was sent out through. It was locked.

A young man kicked and tore a hole through it, and crawled out. A larger woman tried to follow him but she got stuck. Then I passed out. I don't know how I got out or who saved me."

❋   ❋   ❋

Over the course of my investigation I'd heard about workers being crushed by cattle; burned by chemicals; stabbed; breaking bones; and suffering miscarriages and fainting from the heat, fast pace, and fumes. But, according to Public Health Service data, the hidden dangers in meat and poultry packing lay not in accidents, but rather in repetitive motion disorders like the one Betty Jane Stephens had described (see chapter 23). As line speeds have as much as tripled in the last fifteen years, cumulative trauma disorders have increased nearly 1,000 percent.

"I knew a woman who got tendinitis real bad," read another GAP affidavit. "Her doctor said that she needed to go on light duty, but the company wouldn't give her that. Eventually, her hands shriveled up. Her hands were curled into a ball and she could hardly lift her fingers from her palms. When it got that bad, they gave her a job picking up trash outside the plant, but she could hardly do that."

"The company is not impressed by carpal tunnel syndrome," said a poultry plant employee. "Nurses just give workers painkillers and large doses of Vitamin B and tell them to go back to work. When women can't hold a scissors, the foremen give them forks to pick meat off the floor. One woman was kept on the line until her fingernails fell off."

"One of the things that makes repetitive motion problems worse is the cold, wet conditions at the plant," said another. "Particularly in the winter it is very cold, which aggravates the arthritis that sets in. The company won't even let us off the line to get dry gloves when the ones we're wearing—and have to buy ourselves—get torn and soaked. Some brave foremen would allow us to sneak off and get dry gloves. But they would say to be very quick and not tell anyone that they had done it."

"The company makes an example out of independent people," said another. "A woman who complained about her carpal tunnel syndrome and went to her own doctor was ordered to mop the ceiling when she returned from surgery with approval for light duty. One employee was ordered to go out into forty degree rain and pick up all the cigarette butts off the ground."

≈   ≈   ≈

Knowing that they can—and will—be fired for complaints about injuries, illness, and working conditions, employees are scared silent. "Workers come to work injured or sick, or don't report an injury for fear that they will be fired. I was fired because I was out three days with shortness of breath, pain in the wrist, arthritic knee, and bursitis. Although I had doctors' notes for my missing work, the company took the notes but then fired me anyway. I have tried to regain my position, because I have worked there for nineteen years."

"The treatment that we receive is very bad," said a Mexican man. "If we talk for a moment while working, one supervisor told us that he would cut off our tongues. Even to go to the bathroom becomes a problem for us. I am a diabetic, and I need to use the bathroom frequently. I suffer very much because sometimes I need to use the bathroom and I am not allowed to do so. The past month, two workers made a mess in their pants because they were not allowed to use the bathroom even on an emergency basis. We have been told that if we use the bath-room outside of the break time, that the plant doors are open and we can leave because other workers can be hired in our place right away. Sometimes it's worse than being a slave."

*   *   *

Due to oppressive conditions like these, turnover rates in many plants soar. After quitting, thousands of legal and illegal workers recruited from pockets of unemployment end up looking to slaughterhouse communities to pick up the social costs associated with their joblessness and resulting crime. Disabled workers, like many of those above, find it impossible to ever work again. Drained of their usefulness to the slaugh-terhouse, they're cast aside, reminders of a system that places nearly as little value on human life as it does on animal life.

25

Piercing the Veil of Secrecy

This could have been where my slaughterhouse story ended. But, while writing this book, I received a tip from a government informant about yet *another* slaughterhouse scandal in which the USDA was knowingly putting the public at great risk. It involved a secret federal investigation into the veal industry's use of the blackmarket drug clenbuterol.

Clenbuterol, perhaps the most acutely toxic drug residue found in animals slaughtered for meat, is a steroidlike drug used illegally within the veal industry to stimulate rapid growth in calves. It can cause acute poisoning in humans who consume meat tainted with its residue. Symptoms of clenbuterol poisoning include increased heart rate, muscle tremors, headaches, dizziness, nausea, fever, and even death.

Information about the smuggling of clenbuterol into the

United States for use in veal calf feed had been provided to the Food and Drug Administration (FDA) as far back as 1989. Even though clenbuterol had already been the subject of a major international crackdown in Europe, here in the United States, it wasn't until five years later when the U.S. Customs Service received a similar tip, that someone decided to investigate. Even then, despite the dangers posed to the American public from clenbuterol in the food supply, federal regulators tried to keep their investigation under wraps. My informant feared that unless I could expose details of the federal investigation, it was unlikely that criminal charges would ever be brought against the veal industry.

Acting on this and another lead, I was able to uncover government documents that pieced together the details of the investigation. I learned that ten raids had been conducted by U.S. Customs, FDA, and USDA agents throughout the United States at many of the nation's leading veal companies.

Despite the fact that the feds had documented the sale of nearly *two million pounds* of tainted feed, the USDA was allowing clenbuterol-treated calves to be sold to the American public. Instead of alerting consumers to the widespread use of clenbuterol, the investigating agencies—trying to protect the veal industry from what its members stated could be "potential ruin"—initiated a major news blackout.

Concerned for public health, I turned my documentation over to the *Los Angeles Times*. The story was picked up nationally and made headlines throughout the country. In response, the USDA touted a 1994 "study" it had conducted to assure the public that veal was safe. The department had collected four hundred veal samples (out of 730,000 calves marketed that year), tested them for clenbuterol (using antiquated procedures), then announced that it didn't find a trace of the deadly drug.

What the USDA didn't announce, however, but I learned through confidential documents, was that organs collected from the very same veal calves and analyzed at another USDA lab yielded dramatic cellular change indicative of clenbuterol use.

That's when we set out to determine if clenbuterol could be found—not only in bags of feed, as the government had—but also in veal calves being sent to market. Using an appropriate cover, I visited several of the country's major veal slaughterhouses and obtained tissue and organ samples from seventy-one veal calves that had been slaughtered for human consumption. Since none of the laboratories I approached in the United States was willing to test the samples I'd obtained (they feared that finding positives for clenbuterol would be tantamount to taking on the entire meat industry), I shipped my samples to a laboratory in Holland that operates the most technologically advanced clenbuterol testing program in the world.

At a time when the USDA was telling the public how safe veal was, 26 of my 71 veal calf samples tested positive for clenbuterol. The Dutch chemists were startled to have detected more positives in my small sampling than they had in years of testing tens of thousands of Dutch calves.

HFA Director Bradley Miller and I flew to Milwaukee, where the federal investigation was based, and provided our results to the U.S. Department of Justice. Federal prosecutors were shocked—and embarrassed—that a nonprofit organization such as HFA could so effectively do the job that the USDA, Customs, and the FDA could not.

Next, to put further pressure on the Justice Department to prosecute these offenders vigorously and again alert the public to the dangers of eating veal, I called my contacts at ABC's "PrimeTime Live." Since this, like ABC's exposé of Streamlined Inspection, was an issue that hit consumers where they ate, "PrimeTime" ran our story.

Since then, several veal industry leaders have been convicted for their roles in the scandal. In 1997, the first company indicted and its president, both convicted on twelve felony counts of drug smuggling and distribution, were sentenced in federal court. The company was required to pay over a million dollars and its president was sentenced to three and a half years in prison. Since that first conviction, ten more major veal industry figures have been imprisoned and/or forced to pay huge fines. One mastermind behind the black-market drug smuggling scheme, a Dutch businessman with strong financial ties to the U.S. veal industry, is now a fugitive from U.S. authorities. And HFA is currently pressuring Dutch authorities to extradite him to the United States where he faces five years imprisonment and a $250,000 fine on each of three counts associated with the case.

*   *   *

I hadn't forgotten the information that meat inspector-union chairman Dave Carney had given me about the fraudulent statement that appears on export certificates when U.S. poultry is shipped to Canada. At this time, the Humane Farming Association is considering taking legal action on behalf of the eight billion birds that are cruelly paralyzed—not stunned—prior to slaughter in the United States. We intend to petition the USDA on behalf of U.S. citizens living in Canada for the department's fraudulent claims that birds bound for Canada are "subject to humane slaughter and were stunned before slaughter." The statement, required by the Canadian government, is being typed on U.S. export certificates for millions of pounds of poultry shipped to Canada, when in fact, the United States is one of the few industrialized countries that neither requires nor practices humane poultry slaughter.

26

HACCP: A Trojan Horse for Deregulation

"When my child nearly died of food poisoning," explained STOP cofounder Mary Heersink recalling her son Damion's ordeal, "I just thought that we were the unlucky victims of some agency lapse, some innocent mistake, a casualty of the ineptitude that we've been taught to expect from government. I was so wrong. The more I researched, the more I realized that what almost killed my boy goes far beyond agency stupidity. We have an insular, arrogant, reckless, immoral system that now asks us to trust it to come up with the next better idea."

Streamlined Inspection was the "next better idea" for a while. But Streamlined Inspection was only one of many programs that the department had slipped into practice. GAP has records on file that document the USDA's long history of improprieties—from tainted meat scams to the intentional

283

importation of contaminated meat to the deliberate slaughter
of diseased cattle. In one program after another, the USDA's
game plan has always been the same: to reduce government
oversight so that meat packers can push off more bad meat on
the public.

"You go back fifteen years and it's quite obvious that the
USDA has been on a path to deregulate meat and poultry
inspection. And they've tried to do so in a variety of different
ways. Streamlined cattle and poultry are only two of the more
recent initiatives," said former USDA Director of Food
Inspection Rodney Leonard, who then rattled off a long list of
industry-devised meat inspection programs.

"Each time the USDA has tried to convince the public of a
program's benefit and failed, they've gone away and come back
with a different acronym. You don't see the USDA making a
concerted effort to deal with the problems within the agency.
Instead, they keep creating inspection programs to resolve the
problems that the slaughter and processing industries have."

❋   ❋   ❋

In July 1996, President Clinton announced yet another new
USDA meat inspection program, touting it as a breakthrough
in food safety. The new initiative, called Hazard Analysis Critical Control Points (HACCP), requires companies to identify
the major points of potential contamination in the production
process in an effort to prevent contamination, and also calls
for a token amount of microbial testing. On the surface, the
introduction of microbial testing is a great advance, something
consumer advocates have been pushing for years. In practice,
following the tradition of Streamlined Inspection and other

earlier USDA initiatives, the new regulations are a Trojan horse for deregulation.

To start, while microbial testing will be conducted, it will not pinpoint specific contaminated carcasses for trimming or condemning, but instead will sample a small fraction of meat and poultry to ensure that levels of contaminants are within average bounds.* USDA inspectors will no longer conduct daily sanitation checks before slaughter begins. Meat and poultry packers will no longer be required to obtain prior USDA approval for plant facilities and equipment. And, if implemented the way the meat industry wants, plant workers, with no whistleblower protections, will be replacing federal inspectors on the line.

Even before the new regulations were formally proposed, meatpacking executives started lobbying Congress and applying to the USDA to have government meat inspectors pulled from their plants altogether, saying the new system would make them obsolete. The USDA meanwhile was trying to find a way around the Federal Meat Inspection Act of 1906, which requires inspectors to perform carcass-by-carcass inspections. While the USDA was promoting HACCP to the public as an enhancement to current inspection procedures and boasting about having hired a hundred new inspectors, the agency had quietly erased nearly fourteen hundred inspector jobs from agency ranks.

---

*The purpose of this testing is not to eliminate dangerous bacteria, but to keep contamination from exceeding what the industry decides are average levels. In broiler chickens, for example, that equates to salmonella contamination in one in five birds; for ground turkey, salmonella can be present in one out of every two samples.

"HACCP is just another acronym," said Rodney Leonard. "It's just another effort to privatize food safety.

"While Secretary of Agriculture Dan Glickman promised that HACCP would be used to enhance meat inspection, once it was supported by the meat inspectors' union and consumer groups, drafted, and promulgated, USDA's intentions became very clear.

"The point of the 1980s deregulation attempts was to switch federal inspectors from checking food to skimming paperwork. The point of HACCP is the same."

"Like Streamlined Inspection?" I asked him.

"Oh, it's worse than that."

*　　*　　*

Could the meat industry finally be trusted with corporate self-inspection? I headed back to GAP one last time. Their whistle-blower files documented the types of products some of the nation's largest meat and poultry plants had tried to slip into human food channels in 1996 and 1997: red meat animals and poultry that were dead on arrival were hidden from inspectors and hung up to be butchered. . . . Severed heads from cancer eye cattle were switched to smaller carcasses before inspection so less meat would be condemned. . . . Up to 25 percent of slaughtered chicken on the inspection line was covered with feces, bile, and ingesta. . . . In one enforcement action at a single facility, inspectors retained six tons of ground pork with rust which was bound for a school lunch program in Indiana, 14,000 pounds of chicken speckled with metal flakes, 5,000 pounds of rancid chicken necks, and 721 pounds of green chicken that made employees gag from the smell.

Rancid meat had been smoked to cover foul odor, or marinated and breaded to disguise slime and smell. Warm meat or sour product was added to acceptable meat then processed. . . . Plant employees missed hide, hair, ear canals, and teeth in product approved by the facility. . . . Chickens and hams were soaked in chlorine baths to remove slime and odor and red dye was added to beef to make it appear fresh.

The files described meat packed in boxes with fist-sized clumps of fecal matter. Pieces of lungs, rectums, and dead insects had been found as well. . . . Maggots were breeding in transport tubs and boxes, on the floor, in processing equipment and packaging. Workers continued to urinate in a carcass cooler and on the floor while working the line. . . . Sick employees sneezed on product, sneezed into their hands and wiped them off on passing carcasses, and coughed up phlegm onto product. . . . Plant personnel shoveled food directly off the floor into edible sausage bins.

Plant managers repeatedly fought to allow "some contamination," such as feces, grease, hydraulic oil, maggots, metal, floor residue, and rancid meat. One argued that ground meat, returned while on its way to a school lunch program, couldn't have fallen on the floor although it was mixed with cement, gravel, and wood chips. Another plant manager argued that the floor didn't have to be rinsed with hot water after an employee urinated on it. Plant managers made comments such as, "Who cares? This product is going to New York."*

---

*In January 1998, Cox News Service analyzed USDA's 1996 meat and poultry inspection database and found records of nearly 140,000 similar "critical" violations—defined by USDA as conditions certain to sicken consumers—in USDA-inspected plants. Few, if any, plants were shut down for critical violations. ("USDA Meat Citations Ignored," Cox News Service, January 20, 1998.)

※   ※   ※

In late spring 1997, despite the industry's horrendous track record (and the fact that HACCP was not even fully implemented nor its effectiveness known), the USDA made its intentions for HACCP very clear. In a proposal soliciting beef, pork, and poultry plants to volunteer for an HACCP pilot program, the USDA said that it planned to improve the "use of its resources" by taking the vast majority of inspectors off the production line. The USDA called for the "elimination of unnecessary obstacles to innovation"—in other words, federal inspectors—in favor of "industry monitoring." Meat and poultry inspectors, the USDA said, would be "redeployed" to reviewing paperwork and monitoring the transport and distribution of products after they leave the plant.

In Australia, where a similar HACCP system has eliminated government inspection, the media* has reported a dramatic increase in food-poisoning outbreaks and microbial contamination in domestic beef that is as much as *sixty times higher* than that for government-inspected exports.

I phoned food inspectors' union chairman Dave Carney. "HACCP was originally promoted as additive, not substitutive to meat inspection. But as soon as Glickman got the union's support, he did a 180° turn and said HACCP will replace inspectors on the line. Adequate inspection requires both a microscope and a badge. If HACCP replaces the diagnostic inspection that we perform, that's a blatant violation of the Federal Meat Inspection Act!"

The Sunday Age, "Special Report: Our Meat Scandal, New Health Fears Over Reports," May 4, 1997, p. 2.

27

Education and Empowerment

I asked food inspectors' union chairman Dave Carney about President Clinton's proposed $43 million interagency food-safety initiative, announced in early 1997. I already knew that the bulk of the money was earmarked not for USDA inspection, but to teach people how to cook their meat. This, despite the fact that meat scientists and microbiologists now concur that the infectious dose of E. coli 0157:H7 is so low—and cross-contamination is so unavoidable—that cooking cannot possibly solve the problem: an infected piece of meat will dangerously contaminate your hands and kitchen surfaces before you could ever put it in the frying pan.

"Basically, they're saying that the whole problem lies with the consumer?" I asked Carney. "It's up to him to cook the germs off his food?"

"You got it," replied Carney. "It's literally come to the point that yeah, shit, pus, scabs, feathers, pieces of inedible internal organs, it doesn't matter. As long as you cook it well enough, it's fine."

※　※　※

Just how committed are USDA officials to identifying critical control points and preventing potential contamination before it occurs if, in 1997, the fifteen member nations of the European Union (EU) decided it was necessary to institute a ban on the importation of all U.S. poultry? The grounds? Expedient U.S. slaughter methods and reliance on "decontamination" *after* contamination has been allowed to occur, which "compromise hygiene" and pose a serious threat to European consumers.* "If the burden of control is placed on a single preventive measure—such as treating a contaminated product with chlorine to remove bacteria," stated EU officials, "a significant risk remains that the treatment will be ineffective and the consumer will be exposed to a dangerous product. . . . Good hygiene practices must be followed through the production process, just as a chef works in a hygienic way from the beginning to end and *does not rely on cooking to make the food safe*" (emphasis added). Here in the United States, our government tells us just the opposite: to cook our meat thoroughly in the attempt to make it safe.

※　※　※

And what about the animals? Animals, by virtue of their existence, have value unto themselves and certain inalienable

---

*The EU ban remains in effect in 1999.

rights. Still, if disrespect in life is not distasteful enough, today's multibillion-dollar agricultural complex, in collaboration with the USDA, has ensured that the suffering animals endure on industrialized farms is only rewarded by the kinds of atrocities you've read about. If humankind is so grandiose in its dominion over animals as to overlook even the most basic freedoms during life, surely we can't be so insensitive as to think that beating, maiming, and strangling animals is an acceptable precursor to death. That being boiled, skinned, and dismembered alive is an acceptable way to die.

🐝 🐝 🐝

During my slaughter investigation, I learned how easy it is for some people to ride roughshod over the basic rights of others when greed and profit are their only motivating factors. I learned about a debased side of human nature I'd never been exposed to before.

And I'm not simply referring to the kill-floor workers I met. Finding them so forthright to the point where they implicated themselves in their own affidavits, I've come to believe that *they* are also victims of the system: a giant, corporate system that only permits speed and productivity, and penalizes those who would take the time to do the right thing.

The debased humans I'm talking about are the ones who rarely set foot on the kill floor, the corporate managers who never get blood on their shoes but who set line speeds so outlandishly high that employees can barely keep up. It's these greedy supervisors who not only drill into their foremen that production takes precedence over all else, but who demand that their employees *dis*respect life—their own, their co-workers', consumers', and, of course, the animals'—if they wish to keep their jobs.

I learned about government corruption and how a massive federal agency, in collusion with the industry it regulates, could knowingly and intentionally violate the public's trust. I learned how agribusiness leaders from the private sector, appointed to administer the nation's food-inspection program, could wash their hands of their congressional mandates, and instead use their temporary appointments to carry out a secret agenda on behalf of their meat and poultry industry friends. I learned how these same agribusiness leaders could set the stage for deadly outbreaks of foodborne illness and how they could allow helpless animals to be tortured and dismembered alive; how, with meat industry profits being their main interest, consumer safety a lesser priority, and the welfare of animals a nonexistent concern, USDA officials could have created an atmosphere where packers are permitted—if not encouraged—to operate outside the law.

I also learned about the national news media's skewed priorities; I learned about power struggles in the office place; about how easy it is for people in the trenches to become desensitized when they're forced to do something unethical in order to pay their bills. I learned, from my illness, that I—like all the animals I'd been trying to help for so many years— have value just by virtue of my existence and that I deserve to treat myself with love. What an important lesson that was.

And now, at last, after all this time and all the obstacles my slaughter investigation faced, it feels wonderful to finally put these words on paper in black and white, knowing that people will finally read about what's really taking place behind the closed doors of America's slaughterhouses. Like I said before, the more a person learns about what's really going on out there, the more he or she wants to tell the whole world, in the hopes that society will see and, more importantly, want to do something about it. And now I *am* telling the world. I feel a colossal sense of relief, knowing that the responsibility for ending these atrocities does not fall entirely on my shoulders alone. Now you know, and you can help make the changes.

Afterword

Violations at America's Largest Meat Packer

I've been extremely busy since the publication of *Slaughterhouse* in 1997. Since the book's publication, my interviews have run on over 1,000 radio stations across the United States. Newspaper stories have reported the atrocities not only throughout the United States, but also in India, Australia, France, Germany, Poland, Romania, and other countries around the world.

Working with the Humane Farming Association (HFA), I proceeded to document more violations at slaughterhouses. One in particular, an IBP, Inc. plant in southeast Washington State—today owned by Tyson Fresh Meats—was the source of a massive investigation in early 2000. There, I worked with more than two dozen Latino employees, among the most courageous people I've ever known. They all signed sworn affidavits describing how, for decades, they had been forced to

295

skin and dismember *hundreds of thousands of fully conscious, live cows* at the beef plant owned by the largest meat producer in the world. The line speed at their plant had almost tripled in twenty years.

"Workers open the hide on the legs, the stomach, the neck; they cut off the feet while the cow is breathing. It makes noise. It's looking around," said one worker. "Cows can get seven minutes down the line and still be alive. I've been up to the side-puller where they are alive. All the hide is stripped out down to the neck there," said another.

"Their eyes look like they are popping out. I feel bad that I have to do my job on them," explained a third.

"Sometimes they go pretty far. Sometimes they have all the skin out and they're all peeled. Sometimes you can tell they're alive because when you look at their eyes, you can see the tears of a cow. And their eyes are moving and everything. But mainly they just make a lot of noise and are trying to kick," described another.

"I've seen thousands and thousands of cows go through the slaughter process alive. If I see a live animal, I cannot stop the line. Because the supervisor has told us that you have to work on a cow that's alive."

One brave worker shot hidden camera videotape inside the operation. Here are some of the violations of state and federal laws that were caught on tape:

- Struggling cows were hoisted upside down and butchered—while still alive.
- Cows were repeatedly hit with ineffective stunning devices.
- Cows were trampled as workers forced other cows to run over them in the kill alley.

- A disabled cow was chained at the neck and dragged from the kill alley into the knocking box.
- A cow was tormented and repeatedly shocked with an electric prod. Workers were shown shoving the electric prod into the cow's mouth in order to keep the production line moving swiftly.

HFA conducted a press conference and ran full-page ads in Seattle newspapers, and a Seattle television station exposed the violations by running twenty-five segments on the story.

As a direct result of our action and the public outcry generated by the widespread media coverage, the governor of Washington initiated a investigation. As the NBC news affiliate in San Francisco reported while covering the story, "This is the first time in U.S. history that a governor anywhere has called for a full-scale investigation of slaughterhouse practices."

Adding additional weight to our effort was the fact that the National Joint Council of Food Inspection Locals, representing more than 7,000 USDA meat inspectors, joined with HFA in seeking charges against IBP. Never before had federal meat inspectors joined with an animal protection organization in calling for a criminal investigation of a slaughterhouse.

This sent a powerful message to the public, media, and lawmakers. The USDA's own inspectors were publicly announcing that they were unable to enforce the Humane Slaughter Act—and they were calling for state government to step in and enforce the state's humane slaughter laws!

Law enforcement authorities concluded publicly that criminal activity had occurred at the plant. In the words of the prosecutor, "It's pretty clear from the videotape and the interviews done by the State Patrol that there was criminal activity [at

IBP]." Still, he refused to file charges against the slaughter-house, instead blaming the very workers who had reported the violations in their affidavits in the first place! In short, the situation at IBP is not only a case study in the institutionalized abuse of animals, it is also a study in just how far some state officials are willing to go in order to avoid prosecuting the world's largest meat company.

Despite the state's refusal to prosecute IBP, I worked with NBC's "Dateline" on the IBP story for fourteen long months. "Dateline" correspondent Lea Thompson traveled to Washington State and conducted an unprecedented interview with a dozen of the slaughterhouse workers who all admitted on camera to skinning and dismembering cows alive for years. Then the executive producer of "Dateline" decided the story was "too disgusting" and refused to air the report.

The case did, however, open the door for even greater exposure of offenses at this slaughterhouse and others across the United States.

Congressional Response to Slaughterhouse Exposé

For several years, I had been trying to convince a *Washington Post* investigative reporter to write a feature on slaughterhouse cruelty, and this was the case that sparked his interest. We provided that reporter with evidence from IBP, along with numerous documents and witnesses from other slaughterhouses across the United States. The *Washington Post,* one of the most influential newspapers in the world, published a remarkable story, running three photos from our IBP hidden-camera footage on the front page of the newspaper, exposing industry-wide atrocities. The title of the article, quoting one of the slaughterhouse workers, was "They Die Piece by Piece."

Washington Post editors had been nervous about running the story but were astonished by the public's response. Thousands of readers wrote to the *Post* to express outrage, horror, and most of all, gratitude that the *Post* had run the story. The feature ended up being *one of the highest readership response pieces* in the history of the *Washington Post.*

Washington Post readers—including the highest-ranking members of Congress—learned of the enormous suffering endured by animals in U.S. slaughterhouses. The *Post*'s front-page exposé represented yet another link in a chain of events that led to unparalleled public and legislative attention.

The article quoted plant workers who described, as they had in their affidavits, that animals were fully conscious while being skinned and dismembered. Even the *Post*'s own analysis revealed that animals at slaughterhouses across the country were being skinned and butchered while still fully conscious.

Members of Congress were aghast and immediately introduced resolutions calling on the USDA to fully enforce the Humane Slaughter Act. Following HFA's success in gaining congressional resolutions, we filed a formal petition with the USDA. HFA was joined by several other animal protection groups along with the National Joint Council of Food Inspection Locals in submitting the petition.

We announced our petition during a press conference at the National Press Club in Washington, DC, where I introduced to the news media USDA inspectors who stepped forward to blow the whistle on their own agency. The meat inspectors openly

stated that due to faster production speeds and industry deregulation, they did not enforce the Humane Slaughter Act. They
said that animals in U.S. slaughterhouses are routinely beaten,
skinned, dismembered, and scalded while fully conscious.
Along with our petition, we provided a mountain of evidence,
including worker affidavits and videotapes, to the USDA and
generated even more media attention. We made a simple
request: that the USDA station inspectors in those areas of the
plants where they could observe live animals being handled
and slaughtered. Then, in a one-two punch, HFA followed up
with a full-page ad in the *New York Times*.

As a result, and in yet another remarkable sign of just how
far we have come, shortly after HFA filed its petition and published its full-page ad in the *New York Times*, the Burger King
Corporation followed by filing a petition of its own—one
which publicly denounced the USDA for its failure to enforce
the HSA. While few believe that Burger King was motivated
by a sincere concern about animal suffering, we were gratified
that fast-food chains were publicly repositioning themselves.
After all, Burger King, McDonald's, and other fast-food companies were vulnerable because they had long been purchasing
meat from the notorious IBP corporation. To head off a public
relations disaster, the fast-food chains wanted people to
believe that they, too, were outraged by the animal torture
HFA had exposed in the national news media.

Senator Robert Byrd (D-WV) at the time was chairman of
the Senate Appropriations Committee, and today remains one
of the Senate's most powerful and influential members. After
reading about our investigative findings in the *Washington
Post*, Senator Byrd was moved to make an impassioned
speech on the Senate floor.

"Federal law is being ignored," he said. "Animal cruelty abounds. It is infuriating. The barbaric treatment of helpless, defenseless creatures must not be tolerated. . . . Such insensitivity is insidious and dangerous. Life must be dealt with humanely in a civilized society."

His speech was heralded by activists across the nation as a watershed event in the history of animal protection.

Then, acting on his concerns, Senator Byrd secured additional funding intended to be used to enforce the Humane Slaughter Act.

"USDA has the authority to reduce the disgusting cruelty about which I have spoken," said Senator Byrd. "With this provision, they will know that the U.S. Congress expects them to."

In addition to Senator Byrd's appropriation, in 2003, members of Congress directed the U.S. General Accounting Office (GAO), the investigative arm of Congress, to investigate the USDA's enforcement of the HSA.

GAO Discloses More Atrocities

While we've made astounding progress in educating both the public and Congress about slaughterhouse violations, the 2004 findings of that GAO report, in addition to our own investigations, demonstrate that there has been little change within the USDA. In fact, with the implementation of HACCP (see page 283), the USDA used the new industry-based inspection system to permit plants to erect walls that literally sealed off slaughter areas from other parts of the plants, thus further impeding inspector oversight. At the IBP plant we investigated, an internal USDA document revealed that, due to the construction of one such wall, inspection personnel visited the slaughter area on a *monthly* basis—or once every 50,000 cows!

Beholden to the meat industry, the USDA did not use Senator Byrd's original funding to station inspectors where they could observe live animals being handled and slaughtered. Instead, the department hired seventeen veterinarians, which it called District Veterinary Medical Specialists (DVMSs), who were stationed in *field offices* where they had no direct oversight over slaughter practices. While they may travel to slaughterhouses periodically, these DVMSs encounter the same impediments—workers using handheld radios, code words, and whistles to alert employees that USDA personnel are entering the vicinity—that in-plant veterinarians and inspectors do in observing true slaughter conditions. Amazingly, the GAO report concluded that as of May 2003, nearly a year and a half after the DVMSs were hired, the seventeen DVMSs had only made visits to 63 percent of the plants they were supposed to monitor.

Senator Byrd was unrelenting in his commitment to this issue as he appropriated even more funding for enforcement of the HSA. By 2005, Congress had provided the USDA with more than $11 million to enforce the Humane Slaughter Act. The money, according to assurances from the secretary of agriculture to Senator Byrd, was to be used to hire no fewer than fifty new inspectors for the sole purpose of enforcing the Humane Slaughter Act. To date, the USDA's promises have proved empty. Apparently not a penny of that money has been used to hire even one in-plant inspector to enforce the Humane Slaughter Act. The fact is, the USDA had no intention of devoting any of these resources to hiring inspectors dedicated exclusively to HSA compliance. Instead, the money is being divvied up among inspectors who make wholly unproductive spot checks to slaughter areas. *To date, there remains no continuous on-site oversight of humane handling and slaughter activities at the nation's nine hundred federally inspected slaughterhouses.*

The GAO report, issued in January 2004, further revealed that the department's lack of enforcement had resulted in the cruel slaughter of "hundreds of thousands of animals" in violation of the law each year. The most common violation, reported the GAO, "was the ineffective stunning of animals, in many cases resulting in a conscious animal reaching slaughter." The GAO also revealed that USDA officials attempted to mischaracterize these violations as *minor* infractions!

My predictions about Hazard Analysis Critical Control Points (HACCP) came true. HACCP, as readers will recall, required companies to create their own food-safety plans by identifying and monitoring the major points of potential contamination in the production process (establishing "critical control points"). A limited amount of microbial testing would be conducted by the plants themselves and by the USDA. HACCP transferred many meat inspection duties to plant workers and in large part relegated federal inspectors to overseeing corporate paperwork.

In short, HACCP set the stage for additional outbreaks of food-borne illness. Since writing *Slaughterhouse*, the filth and contamination that has flourished under HACCP has resulted in ongoing outbreaks of food-borne illness and subsequent meat and poultry recalls larger than had ever been encountered in history. We've seen recalls of twenty-five million pounds of ground beef, twenty-seven million pounds of turkey and chicken, and a staggering thirty-five million pounds of hot dogs from plants that had long histories of USDA violations. An inspector who attempted to blow the whistle at one of these plants reported seeing "Live flies and cockroaches in processing departments during operations, dead flies observed on exposed product, repeated condensation dripping on product, dried meat particles from previous days' operation, algae growth on walls and ceilings, rusty equipment, and foreign matter in raw materials." Deaths, miscarriages, or illnesses from E.coli 0157:H7 and listeria monocytogenes—a particularly virulent pathogen that kills one in five of its victims—have been associated with all of these recalls.

Inspectors at other plants discovered meat contaminated with ten-inch-long fecal smears, rust, black oil, green hydraulic fluid, pus, blood and ingesta, condensation dripping from rusted beams, and metal shavings—all ignored by plant employees. Equipment was covered with feces, hair, rust, blood, bile, fat, liver and stomach contents from the previous day's operation, and metal shavings. According to an inspector, employees at one plant were working in an area where the drain was stopped up. "The contamination they were working in was slightly deeper than their ankles. This contamination consisted of blood, approximately eight tails, approximately twenty snouts, hide pieces, stomach contents and approximately one hundred portions of the ears."

U.S. Supreme Court Sides with HFA

On a very positive note, legal action by HFA successfully challenged what would—if left unchallenged—have become the third-largest hog factory farm in the world. For several years, HFA has been embroiled in a major battle to stop a massive hog factory from locating on Rosebud Sioux tribal lands in South Dakota. This effort became the centerpiece of HFA's overall campaign against hog factories in the United States. As a result, the public and the courts have become much more aware of the cruelty and environmental hazards associated with hog factories.

With an increasing level of public awareness, agribusiness has sought out locations where it can sidestep state environmental laws and community opposition. Agribusiness is attracted to Native American land for these reasons. And that's apparently why Sun Prairie, a large agribusiness company headquartered in North Dakota, decided to build a massive hog factory complex on the remote Rosebud tribal lands.

The hog complex on Rosebud lands was scheduled to produce a staggering 859,000 hogs a year. The proposal called for another 25,000 breeding sows to be locked in small metal crates.

Despite the fact that the factory farm was to generate more than three times the manure and urine produced by the entire human population of South Dakota, the Bureau of Indian Affairs (BIA) signed off on the project without ever requiring the Environmental Impact Statement mandated by federal law. HFA's first legal victory forced the BIA to concede that it had approved the project illegally. It revoked the lease for Sun

Prairie until adequate environmental reviews were conducted. That brought the project to an immediate halt.

Stunned by this setback, the company filed suit against the BIA in federal court in South Dakota. The company won that round and ultimately prevented the BIA from enforcing environmental laws and interfering with the progress of an operation already under construction.

HFA then appealed the South Dakota court's ruling in federal circuit court and the decision was reversed. That resulted in HFA's second legal victory against this massive hog factory. And this set the stage for the legal showdown that has since resulted in the U.S. Supreme Court siding with HFA and handing the Sun Prairie operation a major defeat.

In the meantime, we stepped up our efforts and gathered additional evidence of criminal animal cruelty taking place within the two sites that Sun Prairie had already constructed and were operating prior to the court rulings. Inside, we documented that overcrowding, neglect, and stressful living conditions had resulted in rampant cannibalism among the pigs. Pigs were being eaten alive by pen mates, their only remains being skin and bones. Workers referred to the remains of these pigs as "rugs." "When you pick up that rug, all you've got is just the skin, the hooves, and the head. And the bones too. The bones may be laying around," described a worker.

Animals were housed in filthy, maggot-infested, disease-ridden conditions. "Shit clogs" in waste pits cause feces, urine, and water to back up into pens with pigs.

Sick and injured pigs were routinely dragged into narrow alleyways between pens where they were provided no food or water and were left to die slowly of disease, starvation, and dehydration. "How long will these sick and injured pigs lie

there without food and water?" we asked. "A week. Depends
on how long it takes them to die. Two weeks," said a worker.
Those pigs that were "euthanized" were frequently beaten to
death with hammers and gate rods. "I've seen people just take
a straight hammer and start wailing on them. I've seen pigs
with their whole head crushed in get thrown into the dead box
and three days later they will still be breathing," said one
worker. "Or you stand on their neck. The way to do it now, we
take the water hose and stick it down their throat and blow
them up, and their butt-holes pop out. We just drown them to
death." Thousands of piglets whose legs became trapped
between floor slats were simply abandoned to die of starvation
or dehydration. Weanling piglets that got too close to heat
lamps were left to burn to death. "We call them 'baby back
ribs' and 'crispy critters,'" the workers told us.

We submitted hours of graphic videotape depicting the
violations, along with eight hundred pages of worker testimony, to South Dakota Attorney General Larry Long, peti-
tioning him to criminally prosecute Sun Prairie management
at this facility. "The fact that pigs have been allowed to die of
starvation and dehydration, have resorted to cannibalism, and
must slosh around in their own wastes is evidence of systematic cruelty," we reported to the media, providing graphic
photos and a copy of our petition to the *New York Times* and
local news outlets. Despite a scathing exposé in the *New York
Times* and additional coverage in South Dakota newspapers,
Attorney General Long staunchly defended the factory hog
corporation and declined to prosecute. We continued to pressure Attorney General Long to file charges against the facility.
Although the pro-industry attorney general has thus far failed
to file appropriate charges against Sun Prairie, we were

nonetheless successful in creating a legal and political environment which made it virtually impossible for Sun Prairie to continue with its development plans.

Between the court rulings and HFA's recent exposés, Sun Prairie has been forced to formally withdraw its plans to operate all but two of the thirteen sites that had been planned for construction on Rosebud Sioux tribal lands! This is an enormous victory, but we are committed to shutting down the two facilities that remain in operation—and by the end of 2005, HFA had filed suit again in federal court to close those facilities down.

Pig-Breeding Facility Shut Down

Once we began making national news exposing the horrific conditions inside the Sun Prairie hog factory, we captured the attention of employees at other factory hog farms. After witnessing HFA's success, workers at other facilities began coming forward to report horror stories of their own. That's exactly what led us to the HKY hog factory farm in northeastern Nebraska.

We obtained hours of videotape, hundreds of video stills, as well as statements from HKY workers and an expert opinion from a large-animal veterinarian all revealing systematic violations of Nebraska animal cruelty laws at HKY. The evidence documented a pervasive pattern of unconscionable abuse affecting thousands of animals. In addition, there existed a potential threat to public health because pigs from this filthy, disease-ridden operation were being sold to none other than John Morrell and Company.

HFA found emaciated sows housed in nineteen-inch-wide crates. Not only were the cages so narrow that the animals could never walk or turn around, but the sows were covered with massive open sores from constant contact with the metal bars. Downed sows that were no longer able to stand were left lying inside crates to die slowly of infection, starvation, and dehydration. "Some of them have problems with their feet. Most of them that die—we took out two the other day—their whole hooves were missing," said a worker. "I don't know if they were caught under something. They had no hooves. The whole thing was gone. Some of them lay in those crates so long their legs rot off. It's just a real atrocity how many sows die in that place."

Newborn piglets that had fallen through holes in the floor to the waste pit below were struggling to stay afloat in feces and urine. "There were like twenty of them down there," reported another worker. "Once they fall in there, some of them were so far in the soup that you could just see bubbles coming up through the manure. And I seen bubbles coming up and I knew something was in there. I could barely just see this one's snout crack through the manure, and I snared him. He did not survive." Next to them were piglets that had already drowned in the liquefied waste.

Among other conditions HFA documented were:

- Pigs suffering from skin infections, swollen joints, respiratory ailments, emaciation, abscesses, hernias, and, in some cases, masses protruding from their abdomens and hindquarters as large as basketballs.

- Overcrowded and stressful living conditions resulting in cannibalism.
- Newborn piglets housed in unsafe enclosures where they became trapped and strangled in faulty gates.
- Pigs forced to live in their own wastes, often encrusted with excrement. Filthy, fly- and maggot-infested conditions, with feces piled a foot high in some pens housing pigs.

We submitted extensive videotaped documentation to the Nebraska Attorney General and to the *Chicago Tribune*. The *Tribune* ran a brilliant exposé, with compelling photographs depicting the wretched conditions we'd documented. Faced with possible criminal charges from state authorities, and with growing national news coverage, officials at HKY were ultimately forced to completely shut down their infamous pig-breeding facility!

The USDA Declares Rabbits to Be Poultry

As recently as summer 2005, another example of the USDA's flagrant disdain for enforcing the Humane Slaughter Act became apparent when we learned that rabbits were being misclassified so the USDA would not have to provide them any protections under the Humane Slaughter Act. Species that the USDA deems to be "poultry" (including the nine billion chickens and turkeys slaughtered each year) are excluded from the Humane Slaughter Act. Astonishingly, the USDA has arbitrarily decided to classify rabbits as "poultry."

This has resulted in nothing short of torture at the slaughterhouse. Our investigation revealed that for some rabbits, this means having their throats sliced open while they are fully conscious and struggling. For others, it means having their necks broken or being struck in the head with a metal pipe or a piece of wood.

According to the USDA meat inspectors, some rabbits are fully conscious as they have meat hooks jabbed through their legs. Workers hang them up by "running a meat hook through the rabbit's leg muscle and sometimes into bone."

Once they are hung upside down, the rabbits have their heads sawed off as they cry out in pain. According to inspectors, workers "use a dull knife and have to keep using it over and over to decapitate the rabbit. The workers were having to try three or four times to remove the rabbit's head. There were occasions where the knife slipped and the rabbit's ears were cut off."

"A worker had numerous scratches and bite marks from the rabbits struggling to survive as he was killing them," the inspectors told us. "The rabbits will cry almost like an infant with loud shrieking noises."

Outraged by what they saw, USDA inspectors contacted their supervisors. They were told that no action would be taken to stop these atrocities "because rabbits are classified as poultry by [the] USDA and are therefore excluded from Humane Slaughter Act enforcement."

HFA ran a full-page advertisement exposing these atrocities in the *New York Times*. The U.S. Secretary of Agriculture was deluged by letters, faxes, and e-mails from outraged readers urging him to take immediate action to stop the brutality that his own inspectors were witnessing. In January 2006, HFA filed a lawsuit against the USDA in an effort to secure coverage for rabbits under the HSA.

A Final Word to My Readers

After over two decades of exposing the violations taking place inside slaughterhouses, as well as on factory farms, we at HFA can clearly see that these issues are now on the national radar screen. Members of Congress, not to mention thousands of people who never saw past the cellophane packages in super-market meat cases, are now being confronted with what sentient animals go through prior to arriving on America's dinner plates.

So when network television executives claim that people don't want to know about these issues, that viewers will quickly change the channel, we can now say, "Give the public the credit it is due!" Americans do care deeply about these issues, and if you give them an opportunity to care, they will show you.

I have seen it in the public's response to the press confer-ences we've conducted, the advertisements we've run, the television coverage of the IBP case. I hear the reaction from callers when I conduct radio interviews, and I know of the unprecedented readership response generated by the *Wash-ington Post* exposé. I have received thousands of letters from readers expressing gratitude for writing *Slaughterhouse*.

I know that reading this book has not been easy for many of you. I am very honored and deeply humbled to have had the privilege to share this information with such courageous readers. I am inspired by your response, and more than ever, remain convinced that we can stop the suffering that so many animals endure.

—Gail A. Eisnitz
Fall 2006

Glossary

Antemortem inspection. The examination of live animals prior to slaughter.

Blood pit. The area of a slaughterhouse where an animal is bled.

Bloodsplash. The rupture of capillaries in muscle tissue during electrical stunning which causes unsightly blood spots in the meat. Bloodsplash hemorrhages are problematic from an aesthetic viewpoint, and thus cause a reduction in meat value.

Broilers. Chickens raised for their meat.

Brucellosis. A highly contagious disease of cattle that causes spontaneous abortion in cows. It is transmissible to humans.

Bung. A slaughtered animal's anus.

Campylobacter. A foodborne bacterium found in the feces of infected poultry. It can cause gastro-enteritis and serious illness as well as death in humans.

Captive bolt gun. A gun, powered by compressed air or gunpowder, that drives a bolt into an animal's forehead to render the animal unconscious. The bolt is then retracted back into the gun for reuse. When properly shot, a penetrating captive bolt gun causes an irreversible stun and the cessation of respiratory function.

Carcass. The skeleton and musculature of an animal, minus the head and legs.

Chain. The overhead conveyor that carries shackled animals from worker to worker through the slaughter and dressing processes.

Chain speed. How fast the chain is moving, measured in number of animals per unit of time.

Checkoff. A government-mandated levy paid by the producer on a per-animal or per-weight basis to an industry trade organization for promotion, education, research, etc.

Chill tank. A giant refrigerated vat of water where up to 6,000 broiler chickens are communally cooled after dressing.

Chitlins. The intestines of hogs used in prepared foods.

Chutes. Enclosed passageways that lead animals from their pens to the stun area.

Circuit supervisor. One of 200 USDA veterinarians with direct oversight over USDA in-plant veterinarians and inspectors at packing plants in a given area.

Clenbuterol. An unapproved steroidlike drug used to promote growth in farm animals.

Condemned. An animal or animal part deemed unfit for human consumption.

Dead truck. A truck operated by a rendering company employee.

Distress kill. A meatpacking plant that specializes in the slaughter of diseased, disabled, and downed animals.

District manager. One of 18 supervisors with direct oversight over USDA circuit supervisors. District managers report to USDA headquarters staff in Washington, D.C.

Downer. An animal that is unable to stand or walk.

E. coli. Escherichia coli, type of bacteria normally found in animal and human intestines.

E. coli 0157:H7. A recently mutated strain of *E. coli* that can cause abdominal cramps, bloody diarrhea, and dehydration; severe systemic illness, *Hemolytic Uremic Syndrome* (HUS); or death in humans.

Freedom of Information Act. A federal law that grants members of the public access to information held by federal agencies. Agencies must provide all requested documents with the exception of those that involve national security, investigations in progress, confidential business information, and other specified exemptions from disclosure.

Government Accountability Project (GAP). A private, non-profit advocacy organization whose purpose is to defend government and corporate whistleblowers.

Gutter. A worker who takes the guts out of slaughtered animals.

Hazard Analysis Critical Control Points (HACCP). A product-quality program that requires manufacturers, in this case, meat and poultry packers and processors, to identify potential points of contamination in the production process, for monitoring purposes.

Hemolytic Uremic Syndrome (HUS). A sometimes fatal illness that usually starts with bloody diarrhea then progresses to hemorrhagic colitis, a breakdown of red blood cells, kidney failure, and other symptoms. HUS is now the leading cause of kidney failure in children in the United States.

Hot shot. An electric cattle prod. Battery or AC-powered pokers that deliver an electric shock.

Humane Farming Association (HFA). The nation's largest farm animal protection organization, headquartered in San Francisco, California.

Humane Slaughter Act (HSA). A federal law passed in 1958, requiring that all swine, sheep, cattle, and horses be humanely handled and rendered unconscious prior to being shackled, hoisted, and bled at a slaughterhouse. The law was amended in 1978 to give regulatory enforcement authority to USDA meat inspectors. The HSA exempts animals subject to ritual slaughter.

Knocking gun. Captive bolt gun.

Legger. The worker who cuts off and skins an animal's legs.

Line speed. Same as *chain speed.*

Meat packer. A company that slaughters animals for meat. A meatpacking company may also process meat.

Meat processor. A company that buys carcasses or large cuts of meat to resell in smaller cuts or to manufacture into meat products.

Occupational Health and Safety Administration (OSHA). The federal agency responsible for ensuring that businesses comply with federal worker safety regulations. In some jurisdictions, OSHA regulations are administered by the state.

Office of Special Counsel. The tiny federal agency that investigates claims of reprisals against federal whistleblowers.

Postmortem inspection. The examination of an animal's head, carcass, and viscera after slaughter.

Render. The process whereby animal parts are cooked down, to separate fat from protein, into a hashlike substance and then sold for use in animal feed, fertilizer, oils, plastics, cosmetics, and a host of other household and industrial products.

Restrainer. A conveyor that transports animals from the chutes to the stun operator. Some restrainers, particularly those used in hog and cattle slaughterhouses, support animals between two angled conveyor belts. Other restrainers, primarily used in cattle slaughter, have a center track on which the animal rides.

Retained. The tagging of an abnormal animal carcass or body part by a USDA postmortem inspector for further examination by a USDA veterinarian to determine its disposition.

Salmonella. A foodborne bacterium found in the feces of infected animals. In humans it may cause flulike symptoms, digestive upsets, arthritis, or death.

Scalding tank. A long, narrow tank containing 140 degree water through which hogs are dragged to loosen hair for dehairing.

Shackler. A worker who places a chain around an animal's hind leg so that it can be hoisted and hung on the overhead rail.

Slaughterhouse. An establishment that kills animals for their meat.

Stick. Severing the major blood vessels leading to and from the animal's heart. A vertical incision in the animal's throat cuts off the flow of blood to the animal's brain.

Sticker. The slaughterhouse worker who cuts the animal's throat open to bleed it.

Stick pit. The area of the slaughterhouse where the *sticker* works.

Streamlined Inspection. A USDA deregulatory inspection program designed to relieve federal inspectors of many of their duties and enable meat and poultry slaughterhouses to increase their production.

Stun. The administration of electrical current, a mechanical blow to the head, or a chemical, such as CO_2, to produce surgical anesthesia, a state where the animal feels no painful sensation.

Stunner. The person who stuns animals before they are shackled and hoisted; or the equipment he uses.

Suspect. A live animal that appears to be afflicted with a disease or condition that could make it unfit for human consumption when its *carcass* and *viscera* are later examined.

United States Department of Agriculture (USDA). The federal department which, among many other responsibilities, is charged with assuring that the nation's meat and poultry supply is safe, wholesome, unadulterated, and properly labeled and packaged. The secretary of agriculture is a member of the president's Cabinet.

Utility man. A worker who is proficient in many meatpacking jobs and can carry out the functions of other workers.

Viscera. An animal's internal organs.

Index

The Humane Farming Association (HFA)

The Humane Farming Association, with over 140,000 members, is the nation's largest organization dedicated to the protection of farm animals. Founded in 1985, HFA has gained national recognition through its hard work and highly successful campaigns.

HFA's goals are: (1) to protect farm animals from cruelty; (2) to protect the public from dangerous misuse of antibiotics, hormones, and other chemicals used on factory farms; and (3) to protect the environment from the impacts of industrialized animal factories.

HFA's programs include anticruelty investigations and exposés, national media campaigns, humane education, and animal protection legislation. HFA also operates the nation's largest farm animal refuge where it provides emergency hands-on care and shelter for a growing number of abused and rescued farm animals.

The work of the Humane Farming Association has been featured on network television on ABC's "PrimeTime Live," "Good Morning America," "World News This Morning," NBC's "Nightly News," and CBS's "60 Minutes." HFA's exposés have also appeared in *Time, Newsweek, People, U.S. News & World Report,* the *New York Times,* the *Los Angeles Times,* and dozens of other major publications.

For further information please contact:

The Humane Farming Association
1550 California Street
San Francisco, CA 94109

Or you can visit its web site at: www.hfa.org